D0805712

American Voyages to the Orient

1690-1865

BOOKS BY CHARLES OSCAR PAULLIN

THE NAVY OF THE AMERICAN REVOLUTION

COMMODORE JOHN RODGERS

DIPLOMATIC NEGOTIATIONS OF AMERICAN NAVAL OFFICERS

GUIDE TO MATERIALS FOR UNITED STATES HISTORY SINCE 1783 IN
LONDON ARCHIVES (WITH F. L. PAXON)

ATLAS OF THE HISTORICAL GEOGRAPHY OF THE UNITED STATES

OUT-LETTERS OF THE CONTINENTAL MARINE COMMITTEE AND BOARD
OF ADMIRALTY, 2 VOLUMES (EDITOR)

DOCUMENTS RELATING TO THE BATTLE OF LAKE ERIE (EDITOR)

EUROPEAN TREATIES BEARING ON THE HISTORY OF THE UNITED
STATES AND ITS DEPENDENCIES 1716-1815 (EDITOR)

CHARLES OSCAR PAULLIN'S

American Voyages to the Orient

1690 - 1865

An Account of Merchant
and Naval Activities
in China, Japan, and the various
Pacific Islands

♨♨♨♨♨♨♨♨

A Collection of Articles from the
United States Naval Institute
PROCEEDINGS

UNITED STATES NAVAL INSTITUTE

ANNAPOLIS, MARYLAND

Publisher's Preface

A lecturer, researcher, teacher and writer who stands between Alfred T. Mahan and Samuel Eliot Morison in the field of United States naval history, Charles Oscar Paullin (1869–1944) devoted a lifetime to his work and published some half-dozen books, on the period from the American Revolution to the War of 1812. Yet the work for which he is perhaps best known, *The History of Naval Administration* 1775–1911, did not appear in book form for more than a half century after it was completed. That work, originally written as a series of fifteen articles, was published in the United States Naval Institute *Proceedings* between 1905 and 1914, and was reprinted in book form in 1968.

Almost as well known to historians and researchers as his *"Naval Administration"* is Paullin's *"Voyages"*, a series of five lengthy papers published in 1910–1911 by the U.S. Naval Institute and now made available in this volume.

It is well known that for nearly two centuries U.S. history and commerce have been closely tied to the sea. There is now a vast national literature concerned with the stirring history of the Navy in war and peace as well as accounts of whalers, clipper ship men, and tanker crews who have braved the seas to support a national commerce. With all the reverence and respect paid to the Navy and the merchant marine, it may come as no small surprise to learn that both had their beginnings, to some degree, in piracy and other illicit practices of the late seventeenth and early eighteenth centuries. In this history of early American naval and commercial endeavors, Dr. Paullin sets the stage with Bostonian pirates, touches on the New England trade in rum and slaves, and points out that some Americans found an especially lucrative trade, smuggling opium from the Orient.

Naturally, as American trade spread across the seas, there came the demand for protection of citizens and commerce. The young

Navy was soon busy convoying merchant ships, subduing pirates, and entering into trade and diplomatic agreements with foreign governments. Much of the value of Paullin's work lies in the fact that in the past naval officers were prolific writers, and their detailed reports of such activities, quoted at great length, give a fresh viewpoint of their operations.

Careful consideration of Paullin's accounts will also reveal another interesting aspect of early naval operations—the almost complete independence with which officers performed their duties. In the present state of instantaneous world-wide communications and direct central control of the multitudinous detail of overseas operations, it is refreshing to note that men who were at times relatively inexperienced and not always highly educated were expected to, and did, exercise tact, diplomacy, and statesmanship in the successful completion of sometimes extremely difficult assignments.

This text has been reproduced from copy printed in 1910 and 1911, and for that reason the footnotes, sometimes abbreviated in Dr. Paullin's own style, may not agree with modern bibliographic usage. In the only departure from the original text, a few chapter titles have been shortened, and the opening paragraph of Chapter 9 has been amended to include chapter references for the chronological recapitulation of cruises previously described.

UNITED STATES NAVAL INSTITUTE

Contents

A Note about the Author

CHARLES OSCAR PAULLIN (1869–1944) historian and nautical expert, contributed extensively to the written history of the United States Navy during his lifetime. He was born in Jamestown, Ohio, attended Antioch College, and was awarded a BS degree at Union Christian College, Merom, Indiana, in 1893. He did graduate work at The Johns Hopkins University and the Catholic University of America, and took his PhD degree at the University of Chicago in 1904.

From 1896 to 1900, Dr. Paullin worked with the Hydrographic Office, U.S. Navy Department. From 1912 to 1936 he was a member of the Carnegie Institute staff in Washington, and during those years he lectured on diplomatic and naval history at Johns Hopkins and George Washington Universities, respectively. Unmarried, Dr. Paullin was until his death a member of the Cosmos Club in Washington. He was a member of the American Historical Association, editor of the Columbia History Society, treasurer and trustee of the Naval Historical Foundation, and a member of the United States Naval Institute. A listing of his written works appears in the front pages of this book.

American Voyages to the Orient

1690-1865

I

Colonial Voyages,
1690-1783

The first Americans to visit the Orient were certain hardy sea-faring men from Massachusetts, Rhode Island, and New York, who during King William's war abandoned their lawful trades and embarked on a piratical career. Lured on by a love of gold and a thirst for adventure, they left their familiar haunts in the Atlantic, crossed the equator, sailed down the African coast, doubled the Cape of Good Hope, and navigated the Indian Ocean in prosecution of their lucrative calling. In the latter part of King William's war, it was no unusual sight to see these roistering freebooters, fresh from a cruise in the waters of the Orient, staggering through the streets of Boston, New York, Newport, Providence, Philadelphia, and Charleston—the ports most frequented by them. They wore a garb calculated to arouse the awe of the quiet citizens, " a broad crimson sash across the left shoulder, a laced cap, a fancy jacket, white knickerbockers, a heavy gold chain, and no less than three or four richly-mounted pistols in a gaudy belt." [1]

Not a few references to voyages in the Eastern seas made by American pirates are to be found in the early colonial records. Concerning a citizen of Massachusetts, a native of the seat of Harvard College, the Earl of Bellomont, governor of New York, wrote as follows to the Lords of Trade in London, on May 3, 1699:

Your Lordships I presume will have a full account from Boston of a parcell of pirates lately taken there with their ringleader, Joseph Bradish,

---

[1] Ulmann, Albert. A Landmark History of New York, 59.

3

born at Cambridge near Boston. The Commander, Bradish, ran away with the ship called the *Adventure* of London, an interloper to the East Indies, leaving the true Commander, Captain Gulleck, on some island in the East Indies, together with some officers and men that belonged to the ship. They came to the east end of Nassau Island [Long Island] and sunk the ship between that and Block Island. The ship of about 400 tons. I had no notice till a week after the ship was sunk, or if I had had notice I could have done nothing towards seizing or securing the ship or men without a man of Warr.[2]

A document of the date 1697, to be found in the Rhode Island colonial records, affords a glimpse of the movements of Captain Want or Wanton, a member of a distinguished family of that colony, and of several other notorious Rhode Islanders. From this source the following note has been obtained:

William Mews, a pirate, fitted out at Rhode Island. Thomas Jones is concerned in the *Old Bark*, with Capt'n Want, and lives in Rhode Island. Want is gone into the Gulf of Persia, and in all probability is either at Rhode Island or Carolina by this time. Want's wife lives there [Rhode Island]. Want broke up there about three years ago, after a good voyage and spent his money there, and in Pennsylvania.[3]

The varied career of Captain Thomas Tew, of Newport, is worthy of notice. He was a friend of Captain Misson, who founded a colony on the island of Madagascar. These two, with a third pirate, a Portuguese, named Caraccioli, established a democratic and representative government for the colony. They were elected by the people, for terms of three years, to the three principal offices. Misson was the " lord conservator "; Tew, the " admiral "; and Caraccioli, the " secretary of state." Slavery was abolished. The coast of Madagascar was surveyed, and an exact chart made showing sands, shoals, and depths of water. A fort, batteries, wharves, and ships were constructed. One piece of land the pirates placed under cultivation, and another piece they enclosed for pasture, upon which at one time three hundred head of black cattle were grazed. With their settlement as a base, they made forays upon the shipping of the Indian Ocean, and especially upon that of the Red Sea. On one occasion they captured, off the coast of Arabia, a vessel belonging to the Grand Mogul, which had on board sixteen hundred souls, including some pilgrims to Mecca and some Moorish mariners. Many valuable

[2] Colonial History of New York, IV, 512.
[3] Rhode Island Colonial Records, III, 322.

prizes were taken and much wealth was accumulated, but finally owing to a series of misfortunes the colony was abandoned. Tew returned to Rhode Island.[4]

The first merchandise direct from the Orient exposed for sale in America was brought to this country by pirates. Arabian gold, pearls from the Indian Ocean, and Oriental fabrics abounded in the chief cities of the colonies. The treasure of Captain Kidd that was seized in Boston in 1699, contained a characteristic assortment of piratical plunder: " an iron chest of gold, pearls, etc., 40 bails of East India goods, 13 hogsheads, chests and case, one negro, and Venture Resail, a Ceylon Indian." Resail was one of the first Asiatics to visit America.[5]

By 1710 the piratical voyages of the colonists to the Eastern seas had ceased, and from this time to 1783 few or no Americans visited those waters. Certain articles of Oriental merchandise, however, continued to find their way to America. From the close of Queen Anne's war until the outbreak of the Revolution, considerable quantities of Chinese tea and chinaware were used by the colonists, coming by way of England, to which country they were imported from Canton, China, by the British East India Company. It was these articles that brought America for the first time into relation with the Far East. Indeed Chinese tea has a direct connection with the American Revolution, as every one knows—a connection that has led one historian, having in mind the resistance of the colonists to the British tax on tea and the Boston Tea Party, to assert that " in this little Chinese leaf was folded the germ which enlarged into American independence."[6]

At least one American product, ginseng, an article highly prized by the Far Eastern peoples for its medicinal properties, was imported into China by the British East India Company. It is said that this company sent agents to the Northern colonies, who induced the Indians by gifts of money, whiskey, and trinkets to search the woods for ginseng. That illustrious divine, the Reverend Jonathan Edwards, who conducted an Indian school at

[4] Johnson, Charles. A General History of the Pyrates, II, 81, 110, 265; Sheffield, W. P. Privateersmen of Newport, 39; New Jersey Archives, 1st Ser., II, 277.

[5] Weeden, W. B. Economic and Social History of New England, I, 345-351.

[6] Weeden, W. B. Economic and Social History of New England, II, 539.

Stockbridge, Massachusetts, was sorely grieved at the demoralization of his dusky pupils caused by the offer of the agents.[7]

At the time of the American Revolution, the seagoing trade between the Occident and the Orient was in the hands of the chief commercial nations of Europe—Great Britain, the Netherlands, France, Spain, and Portugal. Each of these countries had colonies or trading posts in Southern or Eastern Asia. Great Britain was firmly intrenched in India, with Calcutta, Madras, and Bombay as her chief ports. After the Seven Years' War, France still retained a foothold on the Coromandel coast. Portugal held Goa in India, and Macao in China. Next to the English in the importance of their possessions were the Dutch, whose settlements in the East Indies were strategically located. Their capital was Batavia, situated on the island of Java. The Spanish were firmly established in the Philippines, with Manila as their chief city. In the Far East—China, Korea, and Japan—only three ports were open to the European trade, and one of these, Nagasaki, Japan, to the Dutch only, and to them in a limited way. The other two ports, Macao and Canton, China, carried on a considerable commerce with England, the Netherlands, France, and Portugal.

On the outbreak of the Revolution in 1775 the revolting colonies established a small navy, but owing to its weakness as compared with the powerful fleet of the mother country, it was forced to engage chiefly in the destruction of British commerce. Its ships visited every trade route of the North Atlantic, and not infrequently returned home richly laden with captured spoils. Casting about for a profitable employment of its navy, the Continental Congress was impressed with the promising field for commerce-destroying presented by Great Britain's Oriental trade. In December, 1777, its Committee of Foreign Affairs formulated a plan for a naval expedition to the coast of India, which was set forth as follows in a letter of the committee to the American Commissioners at Paris:

As the Marine Committee have already sent some, and will order more, of the Continental ships of war to France, under your directions, permit us to suggest an expedition, which appears likely to benefit us and distress the enemy. We are informed that two or three well-manned frigates, dispatched early in February, so as to arrive at the island of Mauritius

---

[7] Speer, William, The Oldest and the Newest Empire China and the United States, 410-411; Griffis, W. E., Corea the Hermit Nation, 388-389; Macpherson, David, Annals of Commerce, III, 497, 545, 572.

in June, being provided with letters of credence, and for such refreshments or aid of stores, etc., as may be necessary, from the minister to the
French governor of that island, may go thence to cruise on the coast of
Coromandel, twenty days' sail from the Island of Mauritius, where they will
be in the way to intercept the China ships, besides distressing the internal
trade of India. The prizes may be sold at Mauritius. Our vessels had
better call at Goree, then at the Cape, to avoid the vigilance and the apprehension of the British cruisers.

Goree (on the west coast of Africa), the Cape of Good Hope,
and Mauritius were important ports of call for vessels bound to
the Indian Ocean. The " China ships " were the British merchantmen employed in the trade between Canton and British India,
and the " internal trade " was the India coasting trade. The plan
of the committee was not favorably regarded by the commissioners, as may be seen from the following extract from a letter of
Commissioner Arthur Lee to the committee, dated Paris, July
29, 1778:

It has been forgotten, I believe, to mention, both in our joint and particular letters, that we have attended to the plan proposed by the committee
of sending the frigates to cruise in the East Indies, and upon considering
all things it seemed to us impracticable at present. Better order must be
established in our marine, and the ships' companies better sorted, before it
will be safe to attempt enterprises at such a distance, and which require
a certain extent of ideas in the captain and entire obedience in the crew.[*]

The Committee of Foreign Affairs did not urge its plan. The
navy had already begun to decline, and by the close of 1779 it was
not sufficiently strong to undertake a cruise to the East Indies had
it desired to do so. It was left to the new navy established under
the Constitution in 1794 to make the first voyage to that distant
quarter of the globe.

[*] Wharton, Francis. The Revolutionary Diplomatic Correspondence of
the United States, II, 440-441, 673-674.

II

The *Essex* Convoy to Batavia,
1800

Before the Revolutionary War the longest voyages made by American merchantmen were those to the west coast of Africa, where slaves, ivory, and gold dust were to be had in exchange for New England rum. The acquiring of independence by the thirteen colonies opened up a new field for commerce. Scarcely was the ink dry on the Treaty of Paris of 1783 before several enterprising merchants of New York and Philadelphia purchased the ship *Empress of China,* of three hundred and sixty tons burden, loaded her with four hundred and forty piculs of ginseng and some other articles of commerce, and sent her to Canton for a load of tea and Chinese manufactures. Her captain was John Green, and she carried a " second captain " and a full complement of inferior officers, including two midshipmen. She also carried, as supercargo, a young and gallant Bostonian, fresh from the fields of war, Major Samuel Shaw, late of the Continental artillery, and now entering upon a mercantile career. She sailed from New York on her memorable voyage on February 22, 1784, the anniversary of Washington's birth ; and, after touching at the Dutch settlements in Java and the Portuguese port Macao, arrived at Canton on August 28, the only port in the Chinese empire open to foreign ships. Measured on the route sailed by the *Empress of China,* the distance from Canton to the Cape of Good Hope was about sixty-seven hundred miles, and to New York about thirteen thousand seven hundred miles.[9]

---

[9] For information respecting the early American commerce in the Orient, see Samuel Shaw's Journals, the Journals of the Continental Congress for 1786-1788, and the American newspapers for the period 1786-1790.

Eager to increase their trade, the shrewd Chinese merchants welcomed their strange visitors. Major Shaw wrote:

Ours being the first American ship that had ever visited China, it was sometime before the Chinese could fully comprehend the distinction between Englishmen and us. They styled us the New People, and when by the map we conveyed to them an idea of the extent of our country, with its present and increasing population, they were not a little pleased at the prospect of so considerable a market for the productions of their own empire.[10]

The *Empress of China* arrived home at New York on May 11, 1785, after an absence of almost a year and three months. The next ship to visit the Orient was the *Grand Turk,* Captain Ebenezer West. She sailed from Salem, Massachusetts, for Canton in December, 1785, and arrived home in May, 1787, 65 days from the Cape of Good Hope. On her outward voyage she touched at several ports of India, displaying there for the first time the stars and stripes. In 1786 eight vessels sailed for Eastern ports: the *Leda,* of Boston ; *Hope, Empress of China* and *Experiment,* of New York; the *Canton,* of Philadelphia; the *Chesapeake* and *Betsy,* of Baltimore ; and the *Hope* of Norfolk. Major Shaw, who in January, 1786, was chosen by Congress to be consul at Canton, the first consular position established in the Orient, gives in his journal the following list of shipping at Canton " for the present season, down to the 27th of January, 1787 ": English ships for Europe, 29; English country ships for India, 23; Dutch ships, five; Portuguese from Macao, five; Danish, two; Spanish, two; French, one; Swedish, one; and American, five. In 1789, 15 American vessels visited Canton, four of which belonged to Elias Hasket Derby, the noted Salem shipmaster.

All the chief ports of New England and the Middle States became interested in the Eastern trade. Norfolk, Virginia, sent a ship to Canton as early as 1786. The Carolinas, however, displayed little fondness for exploring the new commercial routes. The wealthy city of Charleston fitted out but a single vessel for the Eastern seas. Of the northern cities, Philadelphia, New York, Boston, and Salem were in the lead. As considerable capital was needed even for a single venture, it was sometimes raised by subscription, as may be seen from the following advertisement, extracted from the *Independent Chronicle* of Boston for June 23, 1785:

[10] Shaw, Samuel. Journals, 183.

Proposals for building and fitting out a ship for the East India trade have been approved of by a considerable number of citizens, who met at Mr. Walter Heyer's in King Street, on Thursday evening last. Several gentlemen are named to receive subscriptions, and this is to give notice that another meeting is appointed on Wedn. evening next, at the same house, when any citizen who wishes to become interested may have an opportunity. A single share is only $300.

Many noted American families laid the foundation of their wealth in the Eastern trade. Among those of Boston and Salem that owned numerous "India ships" were the following: Russell, Derby, Cabot, Thorndike, Barrett, Brown, Perkins, Bryant, Sturgis, Higginson, Shaw, Lloyd, Lee, Preble, Peabody, Mason, Jones, and Gray. In 1787, Providence, Rhode Island, sent out her first vessel, the *General Washington,* the property of Messrs. Brown, Francis, and Pintard. Soon Newport, Nantucket, New Bedford, New Haven, and Bristol were added to the list of New England ports trading with the East Indies and the Far East. In 1789 one of Elias Hasket Derby's ships brought home the first cargo of Bombay cotton imported to the United States. In the previous year a Baltimore vessel, the *Chesapeake,* showed the American colors in the Ganges for the first time. When this ship arrived at Bengal the local government was in doubt as to how the flag of the new American nation was to be received, and it applied by letter for instructions to the governor-general of the British possessions, Lord Cornwallis, who a few years before had surrendered his army to General Washington at Yorktown, and who on the arrival of the *Chesapeake* was in the interior of India. Cornwallis replied that the American flag was to be received in the same manner as the flags of the most favored nations, since it stood on the same footing with them.[11]

The merchants of Philadelphia invested much capital in the new commerce, and several Revolutionary naval officers and privateersmen commanded East Indiamen—Truxtun, Read, Tingey, Dale, Josiah, and Barry. Read's ship was the Continental frigate *Alliance,* at one time commanded by John Paul Jones, and sold by the government in 1785 to Robert Morris, the famous financier of the Revolution. On her first voyage she did not let go an anchor between Philadelphia and Canton, passing to the eastward of the Dutch East Indies. There is another interesting connection be-

[11] Scharf, J. T., Chronicles of Baltimore, 248; Macpherson, David, Annals of Commerce, IV, 183.

tween the *Alliance* and the Oriental trade.   In 1789 her builder, William Haskett, built for that trade at Quincy, Massachusetts, the ship *Massachusetts,* of 820 tons burden, the largest vessel up to that time constructed in the United States.[12]   In 1791 Stephen Girard, of Philadelphia, began the construction, for the Calcutta and China trades, of a class of beautiful vessels long the pride of that city.   He named four of his ships, respectively, *Montesquieu, Helvetius, Voltaire,* and *Rousseau,* after the French free-thinkers, thus revealing his sympathy with their philosophical and religious dogmas and advertising it to the world.   The first Philadelphia vessel to visit the Orient was the ship *Canton,* Captain Thomas Truxtun, who subsequently entered the navy and distinguished himself by fighting the only frigate fights of our naval war with France.   On January 2, 1876, the Continental Congress granted Truxtun a sea-letter.   Its quaint phraseology bears witness that our government had not yet declared its independence from the documentary forms of the old country.

Most serene, serene, most puissant, puissant, high illustrious, noble, honorable, venerable, wise, and prudent emperors, kings, republics, princes, dukes, earls, barons, lords, burgomasters, counsellors, as also judges, officers, justiciaries, and regents, of all the good cities and places whether ecclesiastical or secular, who shall see these presents, or hear them read:

"We, the United States in Congress assembled, make known that Thomas Truxtun, captain of the ship called the *Canton* is a citizen of the United States of America, and that the ship which he commands belongs to citizens of the said United States, and as we wish to see the said Thomas Truxtun prosper in his lawful affairs, our prayer is to all the before-mentioned, and to each of them separately, where the said Thomas Truxtun shall arrive with his vessel and cargo, that they may please to receive him with goodness and treat him in a becoming manner, permitting him upon the usual tolls and expenses in passing and repassing, to pass, navigate, and frequent the ports, passes, and territories, to the end to transact his business where and in what manner he shall judge proper, whereof we shall be willingly indebted." [13]

In the last decade of the eighteenth century our Eastern trade gradually increased, and by the time of our naval war with France it had become quite extensive.   During this conflict it lay more or less at the mercy of the French ships of war that frequented the East India seas.   To protect it from them, President Adams decided late in 1799 to send the frigates *Congress,* Captain James

---

[12] Delano, Amasa.   Narrative of Voyages and Travels, 21-25.

[13] Journals of the Continental Congress, January 2, 1786.

Sever, and *Essex,* Captain Edward Preble, to Batavia to convoy
home the American merchantmen intending to sail from that port
in May or June of the following year. As the *Congress* did not
succeed in making the voyage, no notice of her and her commander need be here given. The *Essex* was a 32-gun frigate of 860
tons burden, carrying 300 men. She was built at Salem, Massachusetts, in 1799, by the patriotic citizens of that town for the use
of the federal government. The subscription list for her construction was headed by William Gray and Elias Hasket Derby,
each of whom gave $10,000.[14] Captain Richard Derby, a nephew
of Elias, was appropriately chosen to command the new ship ; but
when she was ready to receive her commander young Derby was
at sea, and consequently the secretary of the navy selected Captain
Edward Preble to take charge of her. Preble was destined to win
many laurels in the coming Tripolitan War and to achieve a standing beside Truxtun as one of the most distinguished officers of the
early navy under the Constitution. He was born in Portland,
Maine, in 1761, coming from excellent Yankee stock. During the
Revolution he served first as midshipman and later as lieutenant
in the Massachusetts navy ; and after that war he entered the merchant service, which he left in 1798 to accept a lieutenancy on
board the frigate *Constitution.* His first command was the brig
Pickering, and his next the frigate *Essex.*

On January 7, 1800, the *Congress* and *Essex* sailed from Newport, with three outward-bound East Indiamen, under convoy,
which proving to be dull sailers were soon left behind. On the
12th the two frigates parted company in a gale, and a little later
the *Congress,* having been dismasted, was forced to return to
port. Unaware of Sever's misfortune, Preble continued the voyage alone. On February 7 he crossed the equator, and a little
more than a month later cast anchor at the British settlement near
the Cape of Good Hope to water his ship and await the arrival of
the *Congress.* Here he found seven British men-of-war, under
the command of Admiral Sir Roger Curtis, and six East Indiamen—three American ships, two English, and one Swedish. He
was cordially received by the British officials at the Cape, with
whom he exchanged courtesies. On different days he dined ashore
with the admiral, the governor of the colony, the commander-in-
chief of the local troops, and the director of East India affairs for

[14] Hunt's Merchant Magazine, XXXVI, 179.

the British East India Company. The captains of the British men-of-war, the United States consul, and General Vandalure, of the British Army, dined on board the *Essex*. On March 28 Preble weighed anchor and sailed for the Straits of Sunda, where he arrived on May 5. His movements for the next two months are best told in his own words, extracted from a letter to the Secretary of the Navy:

I have the honor to acquaint you that the U. S. Frigate *Essex* under my command arrived at the entrance of the straits of Sunda the 15th of May. I watered ship at Mew Island, and was employed in cruising until the 15th when I anchored at Batavia, and was received by the Governor in the most friendly and flattering manner. On the 20th of May I sailed from Batavia on a cruise, after having refreshed my ship's company, made the necessary arrangements respecting the provisions and stores for the frigates, and appointed the 10th of June for the sailing of the fleet from Batavia for the United States. I cruised in the entrance of the Straits for a fortnight, in which time I boarded thirteen sail of American merchant ships richly loaded, the whole of which must have been captured had a single French Privateer of 16 guns been cruising in my stead, but fortunately for our trade it had met no interruption for two or three months; and there being no French cruisers in the Straits, I returned towards Batavia, where I arrived the 8th of June; and finding every vessel bound for the United States would be ready to sail by the 17th, I prolonged the time of sailing to that day. In the meantime I received on board provisions and stores for six months and appointed Jacobus Theodorus Reynst, Esq., agent for the sale of the provisions and stores designed for the *Congress,* with directions to have them sold if she should not arrive by the 15th of July.

On the 15th of June, I delivered signals and instructions to fifteen vessels, being all that were bound to the United States, and all except three at Batavia. The 16th I moved the *Essex* down to Onrust, and on the 19th weighed anchor and sailed with thirteen ships and brigs under convoy, the other two concluding to join me below. The 21st, a Dutch proa came alongside with the master, supercargo, and a part of the crew of the American Ship *Altenamak,* of and from Baltimore, bound to Batavia. She was captured at the entrance of the Straits the 15th by a French Corvette of 22 guns and 250 men, which arrived in the Straits on that day from the Isle of France. Four other privateers were to sail for the Straits after her, one of them a ship of 32 guns.

I continued to proceed down the Straits, making slow progress, with the wind constantly ahead. 22d, anchored the Fleet in Anjer Roads, wind directly contrary and very light breezes, the French Corvette in sight hovering about the Fleet. At 1 P. M. I gave chase to her, which was continued until dark, but the lightness of the wind enabled her to make use of her sweeps to such advantage as to escape, and I returned to the Fleet again. 24th, a Dutch proa came alongside, by which I received information of the arrival in the Straits of a French ship of 32 guns and much crowded with men. The Dutchman that commanded the proa had been on board her the day before, and I suppose she must have passed the convoy in the night, as she stood over towards the coast of Sumatra. This ship the Dutchman declared to be a frigate from France, and which had only touched at the Isle of France. At 10 A. M. the French Corvette in sight approaching the Fleet at anchor under Java shore between Anjer and Pepper Bay, very light winds, almost calm. At noon, the breeze increasing, I weighed anchor and gave chase, which I continued until 5 o'clock in the evening, at which time I had gained so much on her that nothing but its falling calm and the assistance the Frenchman received from his numerous sweeps saved him from capture; had there been only a moderate breeze I must have taken him. For want of wind I was not able to join the Fleet again until the next morning.

I proceeded down the Straits and on the 27th anchored with the Fleet in Mew Bay for the purpose of watering. The 30th one of the vessels left at Batavia joined me, the master of which informed me that the other ship, the *Magnus* of Philadelphia, would not be down to join the convoy as the Captain had anchored her at Bantam to wait for the recovery of a sick supercargo. The 1st of July, having completed their stock of water, I proceeded to sea with fourteen sail under convoy as per list enclosed.

It is singularly unfortunate for the American trade that the *Congress* did not arrive at Batavia, as in that case she could have convoyed the Fleet home, and I might have been left to clear the Straits of those pirates, but now they can do as they please as they have no force left to oppose them, the English squadron having left the station. I fear every merchant ship that attempts to pass the Straits will fall a sacrifice. The necessity of a constant protection of our trade in the Straits will, I presume, be sufficiently apparent.

I am in hopes to double the Cape of Good Hope in ten days with the Fleet; at present I have them all with me. I have granted permission to the Brig *Lapwing* to separate from the convoy and proceed alone, the master of which takes charge of my dispatches. My ship's company have been remarkably healthy; you will see by the Surgeon's daily report our present state.[15]

Preble's fleet of 14 merchantmen were laden chiefly with coffee, sugar, and pepper. Exactly one-half of them were bound to Philadelphia. Two were bound to Boston, two to Baltimore, and one each to Salem, Newport, and New York. Their average burden was about 250 tons. The smallest vessel of the fleet was the brig *Sally,* of 113 tons burden, carrying six guns and eight men. The largest vessel was the ship *China,* of 1055 tons burden, carrying 151 men and 36 guns, and commanded by Captain James Josiah, a Revolutionary naval officer. The other vessels of the

---

[15] Preble, G. H.   The First Cruise of the United States Frigate *Essex,* 95-97.

fleet carried from eight to 20 men, and from two to 10 guns. At this time all East Indiamen were armed with cannon, and their crews were trained to use them.

On August 11 Preble encountered a heavy gale off the bank of Agulhas, on the southeast coast of Africa, and the ships of the fleet were separated. He had previously given orders that the vessels if dispersed should meet at St. Helena. He arrived at that island on September 10. The succeeding events of his cruise may be followed by means of some extracts from the journal of the *Essex*.

Sept. 11.   Brig *Globe,* one of the convoy, arrived.

Sept. 12.   Ship *Juno,* one of the convoy, arrived. Saw plenty of whales and porpoises in the Roads.

Sept. 13.   Hoisted the boats out in the morning, and in at night, as usual.

Sept. 14.   The Ship *Nancy* and Brig *Lydia* of our convoy arrived.

Sept. 15.   Ship *Dominick Terry* arrived. Has lost all her boats and had her quarter galleys stove in by bad weather off the Cape of Good Hope. Watering ship.

Sept. 16.   Ship *Globe* sailed for home.

Sept. 17.   Finished stripping the masts, and have replaced the rigging in good order. The Governor and officers of this place appear very friendly.

Sept. 18.   Ship *China,* one of the convoy, arrived.

Sept. 20.   Arrived the Ship *John Bulkley,* which spoke the Brig *Lapwing* on the 14th of August, which had lost both her masts at the deck. She was thrown on her beam ends by the wind and sea, and cut away her mast to right her. With both pumps freed her in six hours. Capt. Stockley of the *John Bulkley* supplied the *Lapwing* with every thing that was needed, such as spars and sails, and Captain Clap of the brig thought he should reach the Cape of Good Hope very well. He adds that Captain Gardner's Brig *Globe* passed him within half a mile while his signal of distress was hoisted, and did not come to him.

Sept. 22.   Three English ships arrived.

Sept. 23.   Sailed the *Dominick Terry* for Philadelphia.

Sept. 24.   Snow. The *Sally,* one of our convoy, arrived, with Midshipman Brown, John Beard, Moses Harriman, and Ralph Wright, our men which we lent Captain Hall in the Straits of Sunda.

Sept. 25.   Arrived the Brig *Exchange,* of the convoy.

Sept. 26.   Fired a gun. Made signal one. Unmoored at 10 A. M. Hoisted in the boats. Sent Mr. Shed and two men to the *Sally*. Got under way, in company with seven of the convoy.

Oct. 2.   Ascension Island in sight.

Oct. 4.   Spoke the Brig *Anna Maria,* from Bordeaux bound to Tranquebar, under Swedish colors.

Oct. 6.   All the Fleet in sight. Continue to keep the two brigs in tow.

Oct. 7.   Whipped Andrew Knowland, the cook, for striking William Woodbury with an axe.

Oct. 10. Recrossed the line in Longitude about 28° 50′ W.

Oct. 11. All the Fleet continue in sight. Saw St. Paul's rocks.

Oct. 12. Charles Swede, who had been sick ever since he came on board at Batavia, died.

Oct. 20. Lost sight of the Brig *Sally.*

Oct. 31. A gale of wind.

Nov. 2. Sent the jolly boat on board the Ship *Nancy* with a supply of bread.

Nov. 13. Chased and brought to after two shots the Brig *Eliza,* Captain Bullock, from Rhode Island, bound to Turk's Island, 10 days out. Chased and spoke Brig *Harriet,* Capt. Babson, from Tortola bound for Boston.

Nov. 14. Capt. Hale and Capt. Stockley asked leave to quit the Fleet.

Nov. 17. Ship *John Bulkley* left the Fleet.

Nov. 27. At 8 P. M. sounded in 45 fathoms, black and white sand.

Nov. 29. At 1 P. M. Sandy Hook lighthouse bore N.W. 7 miles. At 8 came to anchor in 17 fathoms, the Battery bearing E.N.E., 1 mile. At 7 weighed and made sail for the East River. At 3 P. M. moored ship, Brooklyn Point, East. Unbent courses, staysails, and topgallant sails.[16]

---

[16] Preble, G. H. The First Cruise of the United States Frigate *Essex,* 82-85.

III

The Cruise of the *Peacock*,
1815

The American trade with the East Indies and the Far East was almost suspended during the last two years of the War of 1812. Now and then, however, a vessel succeeded in evading the British blockading fleet on the coast of our Atlantic States, and made the long voyage to the Orient, perchance only to fall into the hands of some British ship of war in that quarter of the globe. The movements in the China seas of His Majesty's ship *Doris* give us a notion of the events that happened there during the war. In April, 1814, the *Doris* captured the American merchantman *Hunter* off the Ladrone Islands not far from Macao and brought her into the Canton river, which channel she then proceeded to blockade, in disregard of international law. In May her boats chased an American schooner from the neighborhood of Macao to Whampoa and captured it within 10 miles of Canton. Fortunately before the captors could carry their prize down the river it was retaken by some American boats.[17]

Toward the close of the war the government at Washington decided to send a small fleet of naval vessels to Asiatic waters to protect our commerce and to prey upon the enemy's China and India ships. The navy department chose Commodore Stephen Decatur to command the fleet, and instructed him to return by way of the Northwest Coast, provided it was found feasible, and to retake Astoria, which post the British had captured in 1813. Decatur's flagship was the 44-gun frigate *President*. The other vessels of his fleet were the sloops-of-war *Peacock*, 18, Captain

[17] Brinkley, F., China, X, 210; Davis, J. F., China, I, 78.

19

Lewis Warrington, and *Hornet,* 18, Master Commandant James Biddle, and the storeship *Tom Bowline,* Lieutenant B. V. Hoffman. Early in January, 1815, these four vessels were at New York ready to undertake their distant mission. On January 14, the *President,* unaccompanied by her consorts, put to sea, but unfortunately she was captured on the following day by the British blockading squadron that lay off the coast.

The ranking officer of the three ships remaining in port, and on the capture of Decatur, the commander of the fleet, was Captain Lewis Warrington. He had served as a midshipman in the Tripolitan War, and was one of the officers to whom Congress gave a vote of thanks for their services in that conflict. He was promoted to be lieutenant in 1807, and master commandant in 1813. On his first cruise as commander of the *Peacock* he captured the British sloop *Epervier,* and for this highly creditable performance received a gold medal, the thanks of Congress, and a promotion to a captaincy. In the summer and fall of 1814 he made a successful cruise again British merchantmen off the coast of Ireland. Indeed, but few officers of the War of 1812 exhibited greater skill and proficiency in the naval profession than Warrington.

On January 23 the *Peacock, Hornet,* and *Tom Bowline* sailed from New York for the islands of Tristan da Cunha, which lie 1500 miles south-southwest of St. Helena. Three days out of port the *Hornet* parted company with her consorts, and being the faster sailer was the first to reach the appointed rendezvous. As she neared it on the morning of March 23 she fell in with the British sloop-of-war *Penguin,* 18, and captured her after a brilliant fight lasting 22 minutes. The prize was so much injured that it was scuttled and sunk. Warrington, who arrived at the islands soon after the engagement, converted the *Tom Bowline* into a flag of truce, and, placing the officers and crew of the *Penguin* on board her, sent her to Brazil.[18]

After waiting 20 days for Decatur, not knowing of his capture, Warrington and Biddle sailed for the second rendezvous, the islands of St. Paul and Amsterdam, situated in the Indian Ocean midway between the Cape of Good Hope and Australia. Nothing of importance happened until April 27, when, in latitude 38° 30′ south and longitude 33° east, they made a strange sail in the north-

---

[18] For the movements of the fleet, see Captains' Letters, Archives of the U. S. Navy Department, XLII, 65; XLIII, 112; XLIV, 27, 32; XLV, 19; XLVII, 2, 17.

east and stood towards it, taking it to be an Indiaman. By the afternoon of the 28th they had approached near enough to ascertain that it was a ship of the line. On discovering its true character, they fled, steering different courses. The *Hornet* was pursued, and was soon widely separated from her consort. She was chased for almost two days, a part of which time her antagonist was within gunshot, but fortunately his fire did little damage. Finally she made her escape by throwing overboard her anchors, cables, spare spars, and all her guns except one. Being practically defenseless, she discontinued her voyage and returned to the United States.

Of the movements of the *Peacock,* after she parted company with the *Hornet,* Warrington wrote to the Secretary of the Navy as follows:

In May we reached the Isles of St. Paul and Amsterdam (our second rendezvous) where we found a letter for us, which had been left a few days before by the *Macedonian* brig, informing us of the *President's* action and probable capture. Here I had intended remaining some time to regain the *Hornet;* but being carried to leeward in chase of a strange sail, we were not able to regain them and were at last compelled by a severe gale to bear up, and on the 8th of June made the Island of Java. From that time until the 29th, we were cruising in the Straits of Sunda, where we made four captures, two of which were burnt, a third was given up to carry 150 prisoners into Batavia, and the fourth released, as from her we learned that a peace had been made.

From the different captures we obtained about fifteen thousand dollars in specie, and gold to the amount of four or five thousand dollars more. We have on board ten chests of opium. The first prize was loaded with pepper, and a few bales of coarse goods, for the Malay market; some of which (as he had no room to stow them away) we distributed amongst the crew, as they were much in want of thin clothes. Of the money, five thousand dollars were divided by me amongst the officers and men.

From Java we proceeded to the Island of Bourbon, where we procured bread and other articles, for which we were much in want, as we were on an allowance of half a pound of bread per man. From Bourbon, which we left in August, we made the best of our way to the United States, touching for a few days at St. Helena.[19]

The vessels captured by Warrington were the East Indiamen *Union, Venus,* and *Brio de Mar,* carrying 161 men; and the British East India Company's cruiser *Nautilus,* carrying 14 guns and 130 men. The *Nautilus* was taken after an engagement, in which she suffered considerably, having 15 men killed or wounded. Among the wounded was her commander, Lieutenant Boyce, who

[19] Niles' Register (Baltimore), IX, 188.

lost a leg. The *Peacock* was uninjured. All these captures were made after the conclusion of peace.

A question of veracity was raised by the varying accounts of the fight between the *Nautilus* and *Peacock* given by the British and the American commanders. The former said that Warrington was notified before the firing began by the master attendant at Anjer, Java, that peace had been concluded between the United States and Great Britain. Warrington denied this, as may be seen from his official account of the engagement:

> As it is probable you will hereafter see or hear some other account of a rencontre which took place between the *Peacock* and the English East India company's brig *Nautilus*, on the 30th of June last, in the Straits of Sunda, I take the liberty of making known to you the particulars:
> " In the afternoon of that day, when abreast of Anjier, as we closed with this brig, which appeared evidently to be a vessel of war, and completely prepared for action, her commander hailed and asked if I knew that there was a peace? I replied in the negative—directing him at the same time to haul his colors down, if it were the case, in token of it—adding that if he did not, I should fire into him. This being refused, one of the forward guns was fired at her, which was immediately returned by a broadside from the brig; our broadside was then discharged, and his colors were struck after having six Lascars killed, and seven or eight wounded. As we had not the most distant idea of peace, and this vessel was but a short distance from the fort of Anjier, I considered his assertion, coupled with his arrangements for action, a finesse on his part to amuse us, till he could place himself under the protection of the fort. A few minutes before coming into contact with brig, two boats containing the master attendant at Anjier, and an officer of the army came on board, and as we were in momentary expectation of firing, they were with their men passed below. I concluded that they had been misled by the British colors, under which we had passed up the straits. No questions, in consequence, were put to them, and they very improperly omitted mentioning that peace existed. The next day, after receiving such intelligence as they had to communicate on this subject (no part of which was official), I gave up the vessel, first stopping her shot holes, and putting her rigging in order.[20]

The *Peacock* was the only vessel of Decatur's squadron that reached the East Indies, and like the *Essex*, did not proceed farther than Java. She returned home by way of the Cape of Good Hope, arriving in New York on October 28, 1815, several months after the close of the war. No national vessel had as yet visited India, China, Japan, or the Philippines, and none had crossed the Pacific.

[20] Niles' Register (Baltimore), X, 58.

IV

The *Congress* in China, *1818-1821* [21]

On the termination of the war with Great Britain in the spring of 1815, the Oriental trade rapidly revived. Within a year and a half 42 vessels had cleared from Salem for the ports of Asia, and 16 of them had returned home by way of various ports of Europe and America, at which they had discharged their cargoes of Eastern merchandise. In 1821 Salem had 58 vessels in the Oriental trade. During the eight years immediately preceding the War of 1812 the number of American vessels annually visiting Canton was 29, during the three years of the war six, and during the first five years after the war 39. By 1820 the commerce of America with China exceeded that of every other Occidental nation, with the exception of Great Britain. The chief products carried to China by American merchantmen were ginseng, opium, quicksilver, lead, iron, copper, steel, sea and land otter skins, seal, fox, and beaver skins, cotton, camlets, sandalwood, and broadcloths. The chief articles imported to America from China were teas, silks, cassia, camphor, rhubarb, sugar, vermillion, and chinaware.[22] On the establishment of the Pacific fur trade, about 1790, China became a great mart for peltries.

To protect our merchantmen from the pirates that frequented the East Indies and to afford our navy an opportunity to exercise and improve its officers and sailors in navigation and seamanship,

---

[21] This chapter is based chiefly upon Captains' Letters, U. S. Navy Dept. Arch., LXI, 110; LXII, 10, 48, 85; LXIII, 68; LXIV, 36; LXV, 7, 17, 30, 90; LXVI, 78, 82, 127; LXVII, 129; LXVIII, 15; LXIX, 70; LXX, 32, 40, 94; LXXI, 76, 94.

[22] Gützlaff, K. F. A. A Sketch of Chinese History, appendix.

23

the Navy Department in the fall of 1818 ordered the frigate *Congress* to be fitted out for a two years' cruise in the Eastern seas. The *Congress* was a 36-gun ship, of 1268 tons burden, carrying 350 officers and seamen. Her captain was John Dandridge Henley, a native of Virginia and a nephew of Mrs. Martha Washington. He entered the navy as a midshipman in 1799, and was made a lieutenant in 1807, a master commandant in 1813, and a captain in 1817. He was one of the officers of the sloop of war *Peacock* when in 1814 she captured the *Epervier,* and later he took part in the battle of New Orleans, receiving the commendation of General Andrew Jackson for important services rendered in that fight. His last tour of sea duty was in the West Indies as commander-in-chief of the West India squadron, dying there in 1835.

Henley equipped the *Congress* at Norfolk, and early in 1819 sailed up the Chesapeake to Annapolis to receive on board his ship the newly-appointed American Minister to Brazil. While he was anchored there the Secretary of the Navy sent him his sailing orders, which were in part as follows:

You have been appointed to the command of the United States Frigate *Congress* to proceed upon important service for the protection of the commerce of the United States in the Indian and China Seas.

You will receive on board, off Annapolis, the Honorable John Graham and family, and embrace the first favorable wind after they shall embark to proceed to sea, and direct your course to Rio de Janeiro, the Capital of the Portuguese Government in Brazil, where Mr. Graham and family will be landed; on this occasion you will attend to the usual salutes and pay all respect to the Government and authorities of the place, and consistent with the occasion of your visit. Make as short stay as possible at Rio de Janeiro, and after filling up your water and taking on board such fresh supplies as the country may afford, particularly for the health of the crew, proceed from thence by the most direct route to Canton in China, report your ship there, and after paying respect to the Government of the place, inform yourself of all the American ships in port, and enter into engagement with their commanders and supercargoes to convoy them through the Straits safely, beyond the hostile attacks of the Islanders and pirates, who infest those seas; and then ccntinue to cruise to and from Canton, and in the neighborhood of the Straits of Sunda for the general protection of American ships and property, taking occasion at stated periods to notify the ships and vessels at any of the ports in those seas of your readiness to afford them protection to certain limits as shall appear to you to be necessary for their safety.[23]

On May 16, 1819, Henley sailed from Hampton Roads for Rio Janeiro, where he arrived on July 3. After landing his passengers

---

[23] Private Letters 1813-1840, U. S. Navy Dept. Arch., 262.

for this port and taking in refreshments, he proceeded on his voyage. On September 2 he made St. Paul's Island in the Indian Ocean, on the 20th he entered the Straits of Sunda, and on the following day he anchored at Anjer Road, Java, where the Dutch had erected a small fort. Here he remained three days to provision and water his ship. Of provisions, he was able to obtain only rice. Water, he said, could be procured in any quantity at Anjer, " but of the worst quality, and very high in consequence of the immense distance which it is conveyed by an aqueduct erected by the Dutch at considerable expense." From this port Henley proceeded through the Straits of Banca with several American merchantmen under convoy, and on November 3 arrived at Lintin Island, China.

Lintin, or Lintin Island, was some 60 or 70 miles from Canton, and lay at the mouth of Canton Bay, some 20 miles east-northeast of the Portuguese port Macao. All foreign vessels bound to Canton came to anchor at Lintin, where they remained until they procured from the Chinese custom-house near Macao a pilot and a permit to navigate the inner waters. Twenty-five miles from Lintin was the Bogue or Bocca Tigris, the mouth of the Canton (or Tigris) River. Near the Bocca Tigris was Chuenpe, the anchorage for foreign warships, and 30 miles from the Bocca Tigris, up the Canton River, was Whampoa, the anchorage for all foreign merchantmen. Here in the autumn and early winter months was to be seen one of the finest merchant fleets in the world, consisting of some 50 vessels and 3000 seamen. The foreign factories were some 10 or 12 miles farther up the river, just outside the walls of Canton. The foreign ships were unloaded at Whampoa, and their cargoes were transported to the factories by means of Chinese junks.

The chief official in Canton, the capital of the province of Kwang-tung, was the viceroy or governor, who was responsible to the Emperor of China, at Peking. Among the lesser officials were the hoppo or commissioner of customs and the poochingsze or treasurer and controller of the civil government. In accordance with the Chinese policy of commercial exclusion and national isolation, the officials at Canton held no direct intercourse with foreigners. A body of merchants, about 12 in number, called the hong or co-hong, acted as intermediaries between their government and the citizens and representatives of foreign governments. They were men of large means, owning extensive commercial establishments with numerous warehouses. They had a monopoly of the foreign trade, for which they paid their government large sums of money. They also gave security to their government for the payment of foreign duties and for the good conduct of the "barbarians" or "foreign devils" with whom they traded.

The factories at Canton in which the foreign merchants lived were owned by the hong. They occupied a space about a quarter of a mile square and consisted of a collection of substantial buildings, two stories high, constructed of either granite or brick, having verandas in front supported by pillars. Each factory consisted of five or more houses, separated by narrow courts. In front of the factories and between them and the river was an esplanade, 50 feet wide, allotted to the merchants for exercising, a recreation that was somewhat interfered with by the crowd of natives that choked up the esplanade—numerous barbers and fortune-tellers, venders of dogs, cats, quack medicines, and trinkets, and a host of sightseers come to gaze at the foreigners. Each factory displayed from a flagstaff erected in front of it on the esplanade the flag of the country of its occupants. Names intended to be more or less indicative of good fortune were given to the several factories. The American factory, for example, was called "the factory of the wide fountains." The foreigners were not permitted to enter the walls of Canton, a city of about a million inhabitants, nor could they reside the whole year at the factories, nor bring their wives there. As soon as the season of trade, lasting from September to March, was closed, they went to Macao, where their families lived.

Each foreign factory and each visiting ship was obliged to procure a compradore, that is a person qualified, according to Chinese customs, to furnish foreigners with provisions and other necessaries. The compradore charged extravagant prices, since to his own large profit he added a considerable sum for his government, which in this way derived an income from each ship, in addition to the regular duties. The transaction of business was often impeded by the officials, and the foreigners were subjected to numerous indignities. As the Occidental trade was highly profitable to the Chinese, they were pleased with the arrival of foreign merchantmen. They extended no welcome, however, to foreign ships of war, especially since the year 1816, when the British frigate *Alceste,* on being denied permission to anchor at

Whampoa, disregarded the orders of the Chinese government and passed up the river, silencing by a few shots a fort and some junks.[24]

The arrival of the *Congress* at Lintin greatly alarmed the Chinese officials, and on learning of it they at once took measures to cause her to depart. Ah, the hoppo of Canton, issued the following order to the hong merchants, who communicated it to the American consul, Benjamin C. Wilcocks, who forwarded it to Captain Henley at Lintin:

An official document has been received from the acting Vice Roy to the following effect:

"On the 21st day of the 9th Moon of the 21st Year of Hea-King, the Tso-tang of Macao, Chow-seiheung, reported that on the 17th instant the Pilot Wang-Mow-Chang stated that on the 16th at 6 o'clock in the evening an American Cruiser, Henley, anchored at Ling-ting. On examining the said Captain, he affirmed that a great many of the ships of his country came to Canton to trade; that of late in foreign seas there were crowds for foreign pirates at every port and every pass, waiting to rob merchant ships which went and came; and therefore he had been ordered by his country to cruise every where and collect information, and now having a fair wind he had taken an opportunity to come hither to get information from the merchantmen of his own country, who had come to Canton. He now waited for the orders of the resident Chief Supercargo [Wilcocks], on receiving which he would take his departure. It is my duty to report these circumstances.

"The number of seamen on board is 350, great guns 50, muskets 300, swords 300, powder 800 cattas, balls 800 cattas.

"The affair being thus, I [the Tso-tang of Macao] (who hold a mean office) repaired in person in order to restrain and suppress the conduct of this vessel. I also wrote to the naval officer at Heang-Shan, and fled with the utmost expedition by a dispatch to inform the encampment at Cosa-branca and request them to select and appoint officers and men to go forth and keep guard with careful minds and not permit the said vessel to approach the inner waters. I (who hold a mean office) have examined and found out that the head of the soldiers on board the said vessel intends to enter the pass on board an English Company's ship (or an European ship). Since the said cruiser casting anchor at Ling-ting is a very different case from that of a merchantman and it is inexpedient to allow her to linger about and create disturbance, I therefore most respectfully request that an official communication be made to the Hoppoo that he may order the Hong Merchants to communicate authoritatively an order to the Chief Supercargo of the said country, urging him to give

[24] Shaw, Samuel, Journals, 174-175; Yeats. J., Growth and Vicissitudes of Commerce, III, 537; Rushenberger, W. S. W., A Voyage Round the World, 393-394; Medhurst, W. H., China, 285.

an order to the said cruiser to make haste and take her departure, that she may not linger about many days to create disturbance. The Tung-she of Macao and the Heang-Shan-heen have written to the same effect.

"On the above coming before me, the acting Vice Roy, it appears that as the said vessel is not a merchantman it is inexpedient to allow her to linger about and create disturbance. I therefore wrote to order the naval officer at Heang-Shan to send officers, men, and police runners to keep a strict watch on the said vessel and not allow her to approach the inner waters, and that she may make haste and take her departure, and go home to her own country; for she will not be allowed to linger about here and create disturbance without involving herself in great criminality; and let the day of her departure be reported. I also write to the Poo-Ching-sye of Canton, to despatch an order forthwith to all the civil and military officers in the districts concerned to keep (in obedience hereto) a strict watch and guard on the vessel and press her departure. Further, I desire the Hoppoo to examine what is going on and to command the Hong Merchants to transfer an order to the Chief Supercargo of the said nation, to order the said vessel to make haste and take her departure, for she is not permitted to linger about here and create disturbance."

On this coming before me, the Hoppoo, I find that the Wee-Yeun of Macao and the Tso-tang both reported to me and that I have already ordered the Hong Merchants to enjoin the said nation's Chief to hasten and order the said cruiser to take her departure as appears on record.

I now transfer the above order to the Hong Merchants that they may enjoin the Chief of the said nation to order and urge the said cruiser to take her departure speedily and not linger about here to make disturbance. Let them moreover examine into the facts and report to me the appointed day for her departure.

Let them not oppose a special Edict.—Hea-King Ui Yein; 9th Moon 21st day.[25]

Henley paid no attention to these elaborate orders, knowing that they were harmless formalities, and that similar orders were regularly issued to all ships of war that entered Chinese waters and were regularly disregarded by them. His first object was to obtain refreshments for his ship. The difficulties that he encountered are set forth in his letters from Lintin to the Secretary of the Navy, from which the following extracts have been made:

Mr. Wilcocks, to whom we are indebted for his indefatigable perseverance in endeavoring to obtain for us a friendly reception from the Chinese Government, informs me, thro Mr. Danagh [the purser of the *Congress*], who was despatched to Canton shortly after my arrival at this place for the purpose of procuring supplies, that after a negotiation of several days and mature deliberation on the part of the Chinese Government, they have in violation of all the laws of hospitality refused to grant the ships a Compradore, or person to supply her with provisions; neither will they,

---

[25] Captains' Letters, U. S. Navy Dept. Arch., LXV, 90.

with their knowledge or approbation, allow us to obtain them in any other way except on the condition of my assuring them that I would immediately after leave their waters, which proposition the nature of my orders would not admit of my acceding to; nor would I, except under the most distressing circumstances, been willing to have gratified them. In my last I informed you that I was then weighing anchor for the purpose of going up to Cheun Pee, the usual anchorage for ships of war, but upon my being informed by Mr. Wilcocks that the Chinese Government does not acknowledge Cheun Pee as an anchoring place for national vessels, I thought it advisable to return to my former anchorage off Lintin Island with the hope of getting supplied with fresh beef and vegetables from these islands, as we have heretofore done in small quantities.

The Chinese, naturally of suspicious dispositions, and who from motives of policy have always entertained an aversion to ships of war coming within their territories, have been latterly roused to a greater aversion than formerly in consequence of Captain Maxwell of the British frigate *Alceste* having fired on their batteries and forced his way up the river to Whampoa, which has induced them to take such measures as to discourage all national vessels from coming within their territories. The British brig *Bacchus* having anchored at Cheun Pee with the expectation of getting supplies was surrounded by their armed junks, by which means they cut off all communication with her and would allow her no supplies whatever, in which situation she remained for several days, but getting very short of provisions was finally compelled to leave the country.

On the 20th of November I received a letter from Mr. Wilcocks (a copy of which I enclose marked No. 5), informing me that there were no hopes of getting the ship regularly supplied and advising my proceeding to Canton in an American merchant ship bound up. Altho I had at that time nearly completed my supply of bread, spirits, etc., I resolved to make another effort to have the *Congress* put on the same footing and to demand the same hospitality that had been heretofore extended to English armed ships previous to the affair of *Alceste,* and others. On the evening of the day that I received Mr. Wilcocks letter, I left my ship for Canton in the American ship *General Hamilton,* where I arrived on the morning of the 23d, and immediately had an interview with the head of the Hong Merchants, Hougua, who appeared extremely anxious to know our business here, the time of our intended departure, etc., etc., notwithstanding he had been repeatedly told by the Consul, and at the same time every assurance given him of the friendly disposition of the American Government, and that the protection of our immense trade was the only object that induced the President of the United States to send the frigate *Congress* to China.

I was tantalized with promises of being allowed a Compradore until the 2nd of December when I informed the Hong Merchants that I should address a letter direct to the Hoppoo in violation of their customs. To this they made some objections and requested that the communication might be made through the Consul, which was done on the 3rd of December, a copy of which (marked No. 4) together with copies of the different Chops, or orders, received by Mr. Wilcocks relative to the affair; for the trans-

lations of which I am indebted to Mr. Meneston, a gentleman who trans-
lates for the English East India Company. Since the Consul's communication to the Hoppoo (previous to which I feel convinced there had been
no correct information carried within the Walls) they have, without making
a reply, relaxed so far in their inhospitable restrictions as to allow the
ship a Compradore, for which a Chop was issued on the 7th of December,
since which time our supplies have been very regular, and I am happy
to observe that the commotion which my arrival in China excited has considerably abated, and I am in hopes to leave them impressed with such
a knowledge of the pacific and friendly disposition of my Government
towards them as to ensure to our armed vessels hereafter a more hospitable
reception.[26]

Having obtained the desired refreshments, Henley, about the
middle of January, sailed for Manila, where he arrived after a
week's voyage. As the *Congress* was the first American ship of
war to visit our future possessions in the East Indies, the following extract from a letter of her captain to the Secretary of the
Navy, dated Manila Bay, January 22, 1820, is not without interest:

I have met with a very hospitable reception at Manila, one indeed which
has far exceeded my most sanguine expectations. The Governor himself
[Mariano Fernandez de Folgueras] professes the greatest friendship for
us, and has tendered his services to render any assistance which I might
stand in need of. Under these circumstances I deemed it a fit season to
effect the repairs of my mizzenmast, which I informed you in my last had
been found to be very defective. After representing its situation to the
Governor and having received his assurances that every facility which a
well established navy-yard could afford towards expediting it should be
afforded me, I proceeded immediately to set it out and entertain the most
flattering expectations of having it stepped again in a very short time.[27]

One of the subordinate officers of the *Congress* has also re-
corded his impressions of this visit to Manila:

Our reception here formed a striking and highly pleasing contrast to the
very unfavorable one we had recently met with in the ancient, but un-
civilized and inhospitable, country we had so lately left. The manner in
which we were received by the Governor was peculiarly gratifying, not
only to our national, but to our individual, feelings. The kindest offers
of a public nature have been made to Capt. Henley, and the officers have
been severally invited and welcomed to his house in the most hospitable
manner. His example, however, has been followed by very few of the
Spanish gentlemen; they, preserving in its fullest extent the proud and
reserved character for which they are so noted, keep aloof and pay us
little or no attention even in their own houses, where we often go to

[26] Captains' Letters, U. S. Navy Dept. Arch., LXV, 30, 90.
[27] Captains' Letters, U. S. Navy Dept. Arch., LXX, 32.

visit the ladies, whose polite attention amply compensates for the rude-
ness of the men.[28]

In March Henley returned to Lintin for the purpose of offering
convoy to the American merchantmen about to sail for home.   In
the latter part of April he sailed again, and for 70 days cruised in
the China Sea and in the neighborhood of the Straits of Banca,
Gaspar, and Singapore, but saw nothing worthy of observation.
After calling at Manila, he again returned to Lintin, where he
arrived on September 9.   Renewing its acts of inhospitality, the
Chinese government denied him the service of a compradore and
refused to issue an order for the transportation to Lintin of stores
purchased at Canton.   The viceroy did not deign to reply to a
letter from Henley demanding for the *Congress* the same privileges that were granted to British ships of war.   Finally, deciding
on bolder measures, Henley weighed anchor at Lintin and sailed
up the bay to Chuenpe, near the Bocca Tigris.   This movement
had the desired effect.   Greatly alarmed, the hong merchants at
once sent down the stores of the ship, and Henley was soon able
to complete the preparations for his return voyage.   Before sailing
he offered to convoy the American merchantmen in China through
the Dutch possessions, but they one and all refused the proffered
aid, fearing to incur the hostility of the Chinese government by
taking advantage of it.

Some recent commotions at Manila caused Henley to decide to
stop at that port on his way home.   It appeared that early in
October the Filipinos had attacked the foreign residents of Manila
and had murdered upwards of 30 of them.   One American was
killed, and the American consul narrowly escaped with his life.
According to one account, the outrage was instigated by the
priests, who induced the people to believe that the foreigners were
the cause of the cholera then prevailing in the city.   Another
account traced the commotion to the native merchants, who, it was
asserted, wished to evade their contracts with the foreigners to
furnish sugar at certain specified rates, that article having appreciated in value after the contracts were made.

Henley found the city in great disorder, and business entirely
suspended.   Before he was able to render much assistance the
cholera made its appearance on board his ship, and he was compelled to put to sea.   After clearing the Straits of Sunda the dis-

ease was got under control, but not until 26 men had died with it. The crew suffered also from scurvy, the scourge of the sailing ships of the old navy. In a cruise of a little more than two years the *Congress* lost 68 men, almost 20 per cent of her complement. Among the dead was Lieutenant William Nicoll.

At Rio Janeiro Henley received on board his ship as a passenger to the United States, General Thomas Sumter, our former Minister to Brazil. A revolution was in progress at the Brazilian capital, a small fleet was waiting to carry the King to Portugal, and Don Pedro was to be left in charge of the government. The city was " filled with people shouting for a constitution apparently without understanding what they wanted." The *Congress* arrived at Hampton Roads on May 29, 1821.

V

The *Vincennes* Circumnavigates the Globe, *1826-1830*[29]

Four years after the *Empress of China* in 1784 rounded the Cape of Good Hope on her memorable voyage to Canton, the ship *Columbia,* of 220 tons burden, Captain John Kendrick, and her consort, the sloop *Lady of Washington,* of 90 tons, Captain Robert Gray, rounded Cape Horn and passed into the Pacific—the first American vessels to enter that great ocean.   They were from Boston and were bound to the Northwest Coast, carrying assorted cargoes, which were to be exchanged for the furs of the sea-otter. After remaining on the coast for more than a year, they sailed separately in the latter part of 1789 for Canton by way of the Sandwich Islands.   The *Columbia* arrived in China in November, and, after selling her furs and buying teas, she returned home by way of the Cape of Good Hope, reaching Boston on August 10, 1790— the first American vessel to circumnavigate the globe.

The first American merchantman to cross the Pacific from Asia to America was the little brig *Eleonora* of New York, Captain Metcalf.   She sailed from Canton for the Northwest Coast about September, 1789, and arrived at Nootka Sound in November, being accompanied with a small schooner called the *Fair American,* which Metcalf had purchased in China and had placed under the command of his son, a youth of eighteen years.   The voyage from our Atlantic ports, especially from Boston, around Cape

[29] The chief sources of information for this chapter are Captain Finch's proceedings during the cruise in the U. S. sloop-of-war *Vincennes* and Masters' Letters, 1829-1840 (U. S. Navy Dept. Arch.), and C. S. Stewart's visit to the South Seas.

Horn to the Northwest Coast and thence to China soon became a popular one, as it was exceedingly profitable. In September, 1790, the brig *Hope* sailed upon it, and she was soon followed by the *Columbia, Hancock, Jefferson,* and *Margaret.* Captain Cleaveland, in his journals, mentions four Boston vessels which he saw on the Northwest Coast in 1799, and says that ten others were to be dispatched thence during the season. In the course of half a century our merchantmen visited every part of the coast of the North Pacific and all the adjacent islands in search of the skins of the sea-otter, the seal, and other fur-bearing animals.

American mechantmen did not long precede American whalemen in the Pacific. The first cruising-grounds of our whalemen lay off the coast of the thirteen colonies. When they had exhausted the whales there, they sought new fields in which to ply their trade, passing, in the course of several centuries, from their home coasts to the West Indies, thence to the Cape Verdes, thence to the coasts of Africa and Brazil, and thence to the Falkland Islands and the east coast of Patagonia. Finally in 1791 six whalers from Nantucket and New Bedford rounded Cape Horn and began operations off the coast of Chile. These were soon followed by others, and the cruising-grounds were extended northward to the equator. By 1812 the region of the Gallapagos Islands was much frequented. In 1820 the "off shore grounds," latitude 5°-10° south, longitude 105°-125° west, were discovered, and about the same time the first American whalers made their appearance on the coast of Japan.

With the arrival of our merchantmen and whalemen in the Pacific, our trade with the ports on the west coast of South America began, and it gradually increased from year to year. In 1813-1814 Commodore David Porter, in the frigate *Essex*—the first American ship of war to round both the Cape of Good Hope and Cape Horn—protected our vessels in the Pacific and captured many British whalers. In 1821-1824 Commodore Charles Stewart established the Pacific naval station, with headquarters at Valparaiso and Callao, for the protection of our commercial and whaling interests in that ocean. Stewart was succeeded as commander-in-chief of the squadron by Commodore Isaac Hull, the illustrious commander of the *Constitution* and the captor of the *Guerrière*. In 1826 a new commander-in-chief was sent to the Pacific to relieve Hull, Commodore Jacob Jones, who sailed from the United

States in September of that year with the frigate *Brandywine* and the sloop-of-war *Vincennes*. The latter vessel was making her maiden voyage, having been but recently launched. She was rated as a 16-gun sloop, of 700 tons burden, and carried 190 officers and seamen. Her commander, William Bolton Finch, entered the navy as a midshipman in 1806, and became a lieutenant in 1813, a master commandant in 1820, and a captain in 1831. In 1819 he gained an unpleasant notoriety by killing Lieutenant Francis B. White, of the marine corps, in a duel fought on Castle Island, Boston Harbor.

In January, 1829, when Finch's tour of duty in the Pacific was drawing to a close, the Secretary of the Navy ordered him to return home by way of the Cape of Good Hope, after visiting various islands in the Pacific and ports of Asia frequented by our merchantmen and whalers. An extract from his orders will show the objects of his voyage:

You will then proceed, after supplying your ship with the requisite funds in specie, provisions, and repairs, to the Society Islands touching at the ports in them where it is probable you will find our merchant and whaling vessels, and render to them all the assistance and protection of which they stand in need, or to which they may be lawfully entitled. You will make enquiry into the state, extent, value, and wants of our commerce, and cultivate with the Chiefs and authorities the best feelings towards our government, citizens, and interests. If you should find that our seamen are in the habit of deserting from their ships, you will use every effort consistent with a friendly deportment towards the natives to reclaim them and to persuade the Chiefs to discourage, by every means in their power, a practice injurious to our commerce and much calculated to impair the good understanding which we are desirous to maintain. It may be in your power to render important services to our maritime interests by removing a source of great annoyance and apprehension, if not evil and danger. Many inconveniences have been felt in some of the Islands from the presence of our fugitive sailors, and injury results to our shipping from the example held out for others to follow. It would be politic to adopt a conciliatory course towards them, should any be found, and by prevailing upon them to enter either on board the *Vincennes* or some merchant vessel, thus restore them to their country, to their friends, and to usefulness.

You will remain a short time, as circumstances shall require, and thence proceed to the Sandwich Islands, visiting the port of Honoruru and any others where it may be of service to exhibit your force. The purposes of your visit to the Sandwich will be similar to those for visiting the Society Islands, and the same instructions will apply to both. Chaplain Stewart has in his care and will deliver to you a letter to King Tamehameha and a few presents from our Government to the principal Chiefs of the Sandwich Islands. You will deliver them to the persons for whom they are intended. Here you will remain from two to three weeks, or as long as shall be thought expedient, being careful during your stay to cultivate the most friendly relations and to procure from our consular and commercial agent and from other sources every information respecting our commercial and other interests which may be practicable.

After accomplishing these objects, you will resume your route to the United States, passing by the Cape of Good Hope, and stopping at the Islands of St. Helena or Ascension, or both, and at such other places as may be found convenient, [attending] constantly to the interests and wants of our countrymen, and procuring information which may be useful. After leaving the Sandwich Islands, if the wind and weather should permit, it will be useful for you to visit the port of Canton where our commerce is very valuable. As this will depend so much upon the state of the winds and weather, it must be left to your discretion.[30]

On July 4, 1829, Finch sailed from Callao, Peru, for the Society Islands. On his way he stopped at Nukuhiva, Washington Islands (a part of the Marquesas Group), which had been discovered in 1791 by Captain Ingraham, of Boston, and had been visited in 1813 by Commodore Porter in the *Essex*. About the middle of August he reached the Society Islands—first visited in 1826 by an American warship, the *Peacock,* Captain T. A. C. Jones—and remained there several weeks cultivating the friendship of the native chiefs. On October 1 he arrived at the Sandwich Islands. Here he delivered to the King the gifts and communication of the President and exchanged numerous civilities with him, the members of his family, and the officials of his government, winning the good will of all the residents, with the exception of the American merchants, who thought Finch partial to the missionaries. From some statistics collected by Finch we learn that 25 American merchantmen and 100 whalers, worth with their cargoes $5,270,000, visited the Sandwich Islands annually. The discovery of the whale fishery on the coast of Japan and the independence of the republics on the west coast of North and South America had greatly increased our commerce with these islands.

In the latter part of November the *Vincennes* sailed from Honolulu for China. She passed through the Ladrone Islands, but probably not near enough to Guam to give her crew a sight of that future possession of America. " On the evening of the 19 inst." (December), wrote Chaplain C. S. Stewart of the *Vincennes*,

[30] Letters to Officers of Ships of War, U. S. Navy Dept. Arch., XVIII, 219.

" we passed the most northern of the Ladrone Islands, between Pagan and Agrigan, at a distance of 15 or 20 miles. Both lofty islands, the last so much so as frequently to be seen at a distance of sixty miles. It was near night when we descried them, and nothing but a dim outline was to be seen against the sky." [31] After a tedious passage of 39 days the good ship anchored at Macao, where Captain Finch was hospitably received by the acting consul of the United States, Mr. C. N. Talbot, and by Dr. Bradford, formerly of Philadelphia. Chaplain Stewart was entertained by Dr. Robert Morrison, for many years the only Protestant, English-speaking missionary in China, and Chinese interpreter for the British and American residents. The officers of the ship received many kind attentions from the merchants, and especially from the chief representatives of the British East India Company. A party, consisting among others of Captain Finch, Chaplain Stewart and Midshipmen M. F. Maury and Stephen C. Rowan, visited Canton.

Soon after the arrival of the *Vincennes* at Macao, Finch addressed a letter to Consul Talbot and Messrs. J. P. Sturgis, Samuel Russell, J. R. Latimer, and W. H. Low, American merchants, asking for information respecting the trade between the United States and China and the advisability of periodical visits by our warships to Chinese waters. Their reply gives in brief form a statement of our commercial relations with China in 1830:

We are fully aware of the kind intentions of the general government in permitting the present visit of your ship of these waters, and feel particularly obliged to you for the communication now under consideration, and for the interest it evinces for the prosperity and protection of our trade. Was time allowed previous to your departure to prepare the documents necessary to reply to your communication as we should wish to do, we have no doubt but what we could exhibit to the satisfaction of yourself and the general government the great advantages to our commerce which would be derived from occasional visits by our vessels of war, attended, as they would be, by increased respect for our national character. We will however briefly observe that the commerce of the United States with China is at present on a favorable footing. We have many local grievances and impositions to complain of, practiced by the local Mandarins in contravention of the known laws of the Empire. These we suffer in common with other nations. [There are] other grievances, delays and impositions peculiar to our flag which are vexatious, but of so petty a nature that we have no doubt they would be promptly redressed on remonstrance at any time, if attended with the presence of a vessel of war. Hence we feel no hesitation in assuring you that it is

[31] Stewart, C. S. A Visit to the South Seas, II, 289.

not only our wish to have frequent visits by our national ships, attended as we believe they would be by benefit to the commerce of this port; but that our national character would be elevated in the estimation of the whole Chinese Empire and the neighboring governments, and that especial care would be observed by all not to encroach on our rights, knowing that the power to protect the very valuable commerce of our country was at hand to appeal to, and that the appeal would not be made in vain.

The American trade from all parts of the world centering in the port of Canton fluctuates in value of imports from five to seven millions of dollars annually, with like exports. We have one year with another from forty to fifty ships in the port. And it is frequently a source of anxiety and disquietude to us to hear of armed vessels of doubtful character cruising in the tracts of our ships, which from their pacific character are without the means of defence themselves, nor any where to look for that protection so valuable a commerce demands.

The fact of your visit, brief as it is, will be known throughout China and the whole Indian Archipelago. Should it be followed by those of other armed vessels observing the same deference towards the customs of China and conciliatory disposition as exhibited by yourself, they will in our opinion increase the respect for our flag, enable us at all times to resist impositions with effect, and have a moral influence on all the inhabitants of the various coasts and islands in the route of our merchant ships.

The season for visiting China may be left at the pleasure of the general government. Our season of business extends from September to March, which would be the best for obtaining supplies, for the health of the crews, and of importance to the commercial interests. At all times provisions can be obtained by a short delay. And generally the shipping of various nations have an excess of provisions which might be had without any delay. The visits would be most influential if made annually, and of short stay in the water of China, visiting Manila and proceeding through the seas and straits usually frequented by our ships.

Men of war visiting China are precluded by law from entering the port. They should not come up higher than Lintin where there is perfectly good and safe anchorage. In a few days after their arrival is reported, licenses are granted and an abundant supply of provisions will be furnished by a licensed compradore. The well known character of American officers will preclude the supposition that any interruption to the trade can arise from their non-compliance with the customs of the country.

We are decidedly of opinion that the fostering care of the general government for the protection of commerce cannot be extended to one of more importance than the China trade, and that the occasional visits by vessels of war will be attended with the most beneficial results.[32]

After a brief stay at Macao, Finch sailed for Manila, where he arrived on January 29, 1830. He was courteously received by Senor Mariano Ricafort, the captain-general and governor of the

[32] Captain Finch's Proceedings during His Cruise in the U. S. Sloop-of-War *Vincennes*, January 14, 1830.

Philippines.   The American merchants residing at Manila were of
the opinion that occasional visits there by our warships were desirable.   Some impressions of Chaplain Stewart, written during his
stay at the Philippine capital, constitute one of the first descrip-
tions of the city and its environs from an American pen.

On the morning of the 26th inst., we descried the Island of Luconia, or
Lucon, at a point fifty or sixty leagues north of the entrance of this bay;
and for the two days following coasted its shore, under the alternate influence of a land and sea breeze, with the outline of a mountainous and
finely variegated country in full view.

The bay of Manilla is very extensive, ninety leagues in circumference,
and the city situated on its southern shore, some twenty or twenty-five
miles from the sea. We dropt anchor in our present berth early yester-
day morning; and are surrounded by varied and beautiful scenery. The
circuit of the bay is too wide to allow of distinct views of most of its
shores; but the outline of the lofty hills and mountains, sweeping round
it, is traceable at most times against the sky—giving to it, as a whole,
much the appearance of a noble lake.

The view of the city, however, its suburbs, and the adjoining country
on either side, and far inland, is full and imposing. The city itself, in-
closed by walls of dark stone, and surrounded by a broad moat, lies on
the north side of the river Pasig, which here flows into the bay, while
the suburbs, containing a tenfold population, lie across the same stream
on the north. The aspect of the two sections presents a striking contrast. The dark, moss-covered walls on the one side—screening every
thing from sight except the red tile of the roofs of the houses, and the
towers and domes of the cathedral and churches—stretch a half or three
quarters of a mile along a green bank and carriage-drive by the water's
edge; while on the other, in place of heavy walls, bastions, and embattled
towers, nothing is to be seen, as far as the eye can reach, but a mass of
huts of bamboo and reeds, of the slightest construction and rudest aspect, embowered in groves of the greatest luxuriance and verdure. The
location both of the city and suburbs is very low—a characteristic of the
surrounding country; but some miles inland it becomes more elevated
and broken, and terminates at last on every side in lofty and beautiful
mountains.

G. W. Hubbell, Esquire, consular agent of our government, waited early
upon Captain Finch and his officers, with a tender of the hospitality of
his house; and it is arranged that the captain, purser, surgeon, and myself, shall take up our quarters with him during our visit.

My friend Lieutenant Magruder accompanied me on shore at two o'clock
to dine at the consulate and to take a first glance at the city. The landing
is by the river, a narrow and rapid stream, with a lighthouse, small and
of imperfect service, at its mouth on the suburb side. A long mole of
granite, with a circular battery at the end, lines the river on the same
side with the city; immediately on passing which we perceived a greater
stir of business than is seen from the bay, the river being crowded on

the side adjoining the suburbs with numbers of vessels of various burdens and covered with boats, plying rapidly in different directions. The walls of the city rise from the water, and extend more than half a mile up the stream to a fine stone bridge, affording the only communication by carriages with the suburbs. Besides Mr. Hubbell, we found at the consulate Mr. King, a young gentleman of intelligence and piety, attached to the establishment, and Captains Chever and Benjamin, the commanders of two American merchantmen, at present in port.

The support of an equipage here is attended comparatively with so little expense, that it is not customary to walk, either on business or for pleasure; and after dinner, at five o'clock, four carriages were in readiness for the whole party, with the addition of Mr. Stribling [Lieutenant C. K. Stribling], from the ship, to take an evening airing. The usual vehicle is a light, low phaeton, handsomely finished, drawn by two small, but fleet horses, under the management of a postillion on one of them. The rides in the vicinity of the city are varied, and of a degree of beauty almost unrivaled; but that most resorted to in the evening is a broad road lined with a double row of trees, commencing at the bridge and following the course of the moat and glacis surrounding the city wall to the beach, and extending along it in front of the city, with an open view of the bay and shipping. Here all the rank and fashion of the place assemble for an hour or more every evening, presenting an animated and truly beautiful spectacle, as equipage after equipage rolls along in a double line—one passing in one direction and the other in another—affording a full view, from the open carriages, of all the dress and beauty of the first circles of society. The ladies wear neither hats nor mantles; but, according to the Spanish custom on such occasions, appear in full evening costume.

This drive is called the Calzada. It is open entirely to the country on one side, and leads past the public parade ground, near the bay. The standing forces of the government consists of 12,000 troops, all natives of the islands, commanded by Spanish officers. Five thousand of these are quartered in the city, and the remainder in various parts of the group. There is a regular evening drill; and about two thousand were now under arms. They made a fine appearance; are well dressed, well paid, and it is said, are loyal and firm in their attachment to the Spanish authority. Two full bands were performing, and I have no where heard finer martial music, though all the musicians, like the soldiers, are native indians of the country.

The airing and the drill usually terminate together—the carriages, when the troops begin to move, changing the rapid rate, at which for the hour previous they are whirled from one end of the Calzada to the other, to a walk, for the enjoyment of the music to which they march, till dispersed at the barracks near the bridge.

Two evenings in each week the military bands perform for an hour in the palace square within the city, in front of the residence of His Catholic Majesty's representative, the Captain General and governor of the Philippine Islands, at present the Senor Rocafuerte. This was one of the evenings; and we drove into the city to share in the entertainment. It is a well built, neat, and quiet town, containing a population of twenty thousand, principally Spanish, or of Spanish extraction; officers of government. and of the military department; priests, soldiers, etc. The streets are regular, and well kept, and the whole style of building that which I have described as prevailing in Lima—the Moorish quadrangle of two stories, with covered balconies from the second story over the street and corridors within. Here the balconies, instead of lattice work of dark wood, consist of large sashes, to be thrown open at pleasure, set, in place of glass, with the inner shell of a large muscle, which, prepared for the purpose, is translucent, transmitting the glare of a tropical sun, in a mellowness of light equal to that passing through ground glass.

The houses of the foreign residents, and of the more wealthy inhabitants of the suburbs, are in the same style of architecture; the first story being appropriated to storehouses, kitchens, offices, stables, etc.; while the second is occupied by spacious and lofty saloons, and sleeping and dressing apartments.[33]

On February 9 Finch sailed from Manila on his homeward voyage, and 56 days later anchored abreast of Cape Town, having stopped only in the Straits of Sunda, to water his ship. He was cordially received by the representatives of the British government in Africa, and later by the British officials at St. Helena, at which island he spent several days, giving his officers an opportunity to visit the tomb of Napoleon. On June 8, 1830, he arrived at New York, having circumnavigated the globe—the first commander of our navy to achieve this distinction, and the second to visit China.

[33] Stewart, C. S. A Visit to the South Seas, II, 299-304.

VI

The *Potomac* Subdues Qualla Battoo, *1831-1832*[1]

Within a few years after the *Empress of China* opened the way to the Orient, American merchants established a considerable trade with the Dutch East Indies. Java was the first island visited, the *Empress of China* having stopped there on her way to Canton. The adjacent island of Sumatra was doubtless the next to attract the attention of our shipmasters. Trade with it was begun in 1789 by Captain Jonathan Barnes, of Salem, commander of the brig *Cadet,* who in that year arrived at Boston with a cargo of pepper, spices, and camphor. The traffic in pepper with the Sumatrans soon became quite extensive, and in 1802 no less than 30 American merchantmen visited the island. Salem led its competitors, Boston, New York, and Philadelphia, in the pepper trade. Her shipmasters prepared charts and sailing directions for the coast of Sumatra which were used by both the merchant and national marine.[2]

Among the Sumatran ports most frequented was Quallah Battoo, situated on the west coast in the kingdom of Acheen, a part of the island that had not been brought under subjection by the

[1] This chapter is based chiefly on Letters to Officers of Ships of War, XX, 6-15; Captains' Letters, CLXVI, 73, 74; CXCIII, 78; Francis Warriner's Cruise of the United States Frigate *Potomac;* and J. N. Reynold's Voyage of the United States Frigate *Potomac.* See also American State Papers, Naval Affairs, IV, 150-158.
[2] Felt, J. B., Annals of Salem, II, 294; Trow, C. E., The Old Shipmasters of Salem, 138-139; Reynolds, J. N., Voyage of the United States Frigate *Potomac,* 201.

Dutch. Quallah Battoo was governed by local rajahs, who were practically independent of their suzerain, the King of Acheen. It contained about 1100 inhabitants, and was defended by several small forts. The Quallah Battooans were described as a treacherous and warlike people, much given to piracy. They were no more crafty, however, than certain American traders, who were wont to use quicksilver in their hollow scale-beams, and who would slip ashore at night and fill up their hollow scale-weights with lead or shot.

Toward the end of the year 1830 Captain Charles M. Endicott arrived at Quallah Battoo in the Salem vessel *Friendship,* and having purchased a considerable quantity of pepper began loading it on board his vessel, a mile or two distant from the weighing place on shore. On the morning of February 7, 1831, Endicott, his second mate, and four of his sailors went ashore to weigh pepper, leaving the first officer and the rest of the crew on board to receive it. Early in the afternoon a boat loaded with pepper and manned by Malays was dispatched to the ship. Instead of proceeding directly to their destination, the treacherous boatmen, in accordance with a prearranged plan, ran their craft into the high grass and exchanged places with a band of armed desperadoes, who on reaching the ship clambered on board and without much difficulty captured it, killing the first officer and two seamen and wounding three others. Four seamen escaped by jumping overboard and swimming ashore.

Meantime Endicott and his party, discovering that the movements of the boatmen were suspicious and suspecting treachery, managed to reach their remaining boat and push off from the landing place before they were attacked by the hostile natives in hot pursuit of them. When half a boat's length from the shore, they were unexpectedly joined by Po Adam, a neighboring rajah of considerable wealth and influence and a friend of the Americans. " What, do you come, too, Adam? " said Endicott. " Yes," was his reply, " if they kill you, they must kill me first, captain." On shore crowds of Malays had assembled, brandishing their weapons; and a ferry-boat, with eight or ten men on board, armed with spears and creeses started in chase of the retreating Americans, who perceiving that they would be overtaken, boldly turned about and pulled toward their antagonists presenting the sword of Adam, their only weapon. This audacious movement so alarmed the pursuers that they kept their distance and permitted Endicott to escape. When he came in full view of his ship he found the Malays in complete possession of her. As he was practically without weapons, and three native boats were descried pulling toward him, he decided not to undertake the recapture of the ship until he obtained aid. Rowing to the adjacent port of Muckie, 25 miles distant, he found there three American merchantmen, the captains of which on hearing his story agreed to give him their assistance. Accompanied by Endicott, they sailed for Quallah Battoo and on arriving there demanded the peaceful surrender of the *Friendship*. The rajah in authority positively refused to give up his prize, sending word they might take it if they could. On receiving this message the three captains opened fire upon the vessel and the Malay boats that were still carrying away plunder, and were answered by the guns of the vessel and the forts on shore. Finally they sent a boarding party to take possession of the *Friendship,* which it easily did, the Malays deserting her as it approached. She had been plundered of her specie, opium, stores, provisions, nautical instruments, and clothing.

When the news of the outrage on the *Friendship* reached the United States in the summer of 1831, several merchant captains appealed to President Jackson for protection, saying that the conduct of the Sumatrans toward their countrymen was becoming more and more treacherous, that captains and supercargoes were detained on shore and extravagant sums demanded for their ransom, and that during the 40 years that Americans had traded with the island not one of our national vessels had visited it. The President at once decided to send the frigate *Potomac* to Quallah Battoo to obtain redress for the wrongs perpetrated on our citizens.

The *Potomac* at this time was at New York, under orders to convey Martin Van Buren, minister to the court of St. James, to England, and thence proceed to the Pacific station. She was a 44-gun frigate of 1726 tons burden, carrying 400 men. Her commander, Commodore John Downes, had been recently chosen to command the Pacific squadron. He had entered the navy in 1802, had seen important service in the War of 1812 under Commodore Porter during that officer's noted cruise against British whalers, and later had served on both the Mediterranean and Pacific Stations. His tour of duty as commander-in-chief of the

Pacific squadron was his last service at sea. Certain words written by him in 1833, respecting the importance of this squadron have an almost prophetic significance: "Everything conspires to render the Pacific of great interest to the people of the United States at the present time. Our future sea fights are as likely to take place here as on the Atlantic Ocean, for here we are acquiring a preponderating commercial interest, and here must be our navy also." [3]

Downes's instructions from the Department directed him to proceed to the Pacific Station by way of the Cape of Good Hope, Quallah Battoo, Batavia, and Canton. At Quallah Battoo he was to obtain information respecting the attack on the *Friendship,* and, if it agreed substantially with the account received by the Department, he was to demand restitution of the property plundered from the ship, an idemnity for the injury done to her, and the punishment of those concerned in the murder of her crew. Should satisfaction be refused, he was to vindicate our rights by seizing the murderers, retaking the stolen property, and destroying the vessels, forts, and dwellings of the town.

Downes sailed from Sandy Hook on August 26, 1831, and after a passage of 50 days arrived at Rio Janeiro where he took in water and provisions. At the Cape of Good Hope, his next stop, he learned much from the British officers respecting the character of the Quallah Battooans, who were represented as the chief pirates of Sumatra, brave and treacherous men, by no means to be despised as enemies. This information caused him to depart somewhat from his orders, being of the opinion that to carry them out strictly would defeat the main object of the expedition. He decided to make a sudden descent upon the natives, surround their forts, and prevent the flight of the rajahs. He, therefore, approached the town disguised as an East Indiaman, having concealed the guns and closed the ports of his ship. For the events immediately following his arrival the narrative of Francis Warriner, the schoolmaster of the *Potomac,* may be quoted:

At noon on the fifth instant [February, 1832], we hoisted the Danish national flag, and about two o'clock came to anchor off the town, after a passage of 55 days from the Cape of Good Hope. We came to in merchantman style, a few men being sent aloft, dressed in red and blue flannel shirts, and one top-sail being clewed up and furled at a time. We

[3] Captains' Letters, CLXXXI, 67.

were all anxious to obtain a glimpse of the place and of the adjacent scenery, but no person was allowed to gratify his curiosity in this respect, for fear of disclosing our true character to the natives. Not a single breeze fanned us. Every port being closed, the air that we breathed was close and stifled. The melted tar fell in drops upon the deck, and fairly broiled from the seams between the planks. We were obliged to preserve the stricktest silence, and our situation remained, as it had been for several days, uncomfortable in the extreme.

About four o'clock, Commodore Downes sent a party ashore for the purpose of reconnoitering the place. This party consisted of our first lieutenant, Mr. Shubrick; first lieutenant of marines, Mr. Edson; Lieutenants Pinkham, Hoff, and Ingersoll; acting Sailing-master Totten, and Passed Midshipman Tooley. They left the ship under pretence of contracting for a cargo of pepper. Mr. Shubrick went as captain of the ship, Mr. Edson as supercargo. The remainder in the capacity of common sailors to pull the boat, and they were dressed in a manner conformable to the different characters they assumed. They were obliged to smear their pantaloons with tar, and to stain their hands with rhubarb, that they might resemble old weather-beaten sailors. Their real design was to examine the relative position of the different forts, previous to making the intended attack. When all had approached within a few yards of the beach, they found it lined with a large body of men, exhibiting a warlike appearance, armed with javelins, creeses, cleavers, and sabres, and manifesting very hostile intentions. They, therefore, did not deem it prudent to land. Mr. Shubrick inquired for the rajah. They replied, " He no come down, he be one so great man." Mr. Edson next questioned them as to the price of pepper. They said, eight dollars per picul; but he finally succeeded in inducing them to lower the price to four dollars. A small number were invited to come down to them, and after a consultation was held, about half a dozen approached. Our officers finding that it was their intention to surround the boat, and apprehending some hostile design, pushed farther out to sea. The Malays then exclaimed, " What for you no come ashore?" An excuse was offered, and they were finally told that the next day the captain would come on shore and complete a bargain with them. They inquired with what cargo our ship was freighted and were informed that it was with opium. The gentlemen shortly afterwards returned to the ship, having obtained but an imperfect knowledge of the place, and without ascertaining anything relative to the most advantageous method of assailing the forts.

During the absence of the party ashore, four Malay fishermen, attracted by the sight of an old clump of an Indiaman, as they supposed our ship to be, came alongside to sell their fish. Mr. Barry, who could converse a little in the Malay language, invited them on board. One came up with a couple of fish in his hand, but as soon as he reached the gangway, and saw our formidable battery and about 500 men thickly stowed together, he dropped his fish in the utmost consternation, hurried back to the boat, and gave the alarm to his three companions. They were then told not to be afraid to come on board, that we would buy their fish, and that no harm should befall them. But they were not to be caught in such a manner. They had no idea of becoming prisoners on board of a ship of war, and began hastily to paddle off. Fearing they might give the alarm on shore, a mizzen-top-man instantly leaped through one of the ports into the boat, and seized them. They set up a yell and made some resistance, but a rope was instantly let down, and they, finding that they were about to be dragged into the ship, *nolens volens,* through one of the ports, thought it policy to submit. As they came over the gangway, they trembled; and lifting their eyes and clasped hand to heaven, like men not knowing where they were, cried aloud, "Allah!" in an imploring tone of voice. They were the poorest, smoke-dried specimens of human nature that we had seen, but perhaps more deserving our commiseration than ridicule. . . . .

"Our ship now presented a busy scene. It was determined to commence an attack upon the town the next morning, and every necessary preparation was accordingly made. Muskets were cleaned, cartridge-boxes buckled on, cutlasses examined and put in order, etc. During the evening, the commodore sent for the officers commanding the several divisions, and gave them their instructions. They were ordered to land, surround the town and forts, and demand indemnity for the outrage committed upon the *Friendship,* with the punishment of those concerned in the barbarous massacre of her crew; but were directed to spare the women and children. I had some conversation with a few of the junior officers, upon the subject of the perilous enterprise in which they were about to embark. They felt that it would not be so much a matter of jest as they had been disposed to think it might be. There was some shrinking at the thought of impending danger. . . . .

At eight bells (12 o'clock at night) all hands were called. Those assigned to take part in the expedition were mustered, when Lieutenant Shubrick, the commander of the detachment, gave them special orders. No man was to utter a word after he had entered the boat; no one was to fire till the command was given; and no man was to desert his ranks. Considerable time was occupied in getting the men into the boats, and in making all things ready. Several of the officers felt impatient at the delay and were fearful that they would be unable to effect a landing in season to surprise the enemy. At length the gallant band, to the number of 282 men—including officers, left the ship about two o'clock.[4]

The landing party was commanded by the first lieutenant of the *Potomac,* Irvine Shubrick, and was divided into four divisions —three of seamen and one of marines. The first division of seamen was commanded by Lieutenant R. R. Pinkham; the second, by Lieutenant Henry Hoff; and the third, by Lieutenant Jonathan Ingersoll. The division of the last named was strengthened by a piece of artillery, a 6-pounder called the Betsey Baker, in command of Sailing-master R. S. Totten. A company of marines, commanded by Lieutenants Alvin Edson and G. H. Terrett, con-

[4] Warriner, Francis. Cruise of the United States Frigate *Potomac,* 77-84.

stituted the fourth division. The capture of a fort was assigned to each division. Mr. John Barry, of Salem, formerly the second officer of the *Friendship,* and now master's mate of the *Potomac,* acted as guide. Commodore Downes remained on board throughout the engagement, taking a station at the larboard gangway, with a spy-glass in his hand. At times, however, he was on the point of running in closer with his ship to aid the landing party. The officers and crew on board took up positions in various quarters, some in the tops, and some hanging upon the shrouds, others in the rigging, and still others on the Jacob's ladder, all " gazing with breathless anxiety." Let us return to Warriner's narrative:

It seems our party had effected a landing near the dawn of day, amid a heavy surf, about a mile and a half to the north of the town, undiscovered by the enemy, and without any serious accident having befallen them; though several of the party were thoroughly drenched by the beating of the surf, and some of their ammunition was injured. The troops were then drawn up in regular order, and under the chief command of Lieutenant Shubrick, took up their line of march against the enemy, over a beach of deep and heavy sand. They had not proceeded far, before they were discovered by a native at a distance, who ran at full speed to give the alarm. The lieutenant ordered his men to quicken their pace, to press onward, and, if possible, to take possession of the forts, ere the enemy should be apprised of the approach. A rapid march soon brought them up with the first fort, when a division of men under the command of Lieutenant Hoff, was detached from the main body, and ordered to surround it. By the time the detachment had reached the rear of the fort, the remainder of the forces had gained its front, and were passing it on their march to assail the other forts, when a shower of balls from some quarter passed over their heads.

The first fort had been found difficult of access, in consequence of a deep hedge of thorn-bushes and brambles with which it was environed. The assault was commenced by the pioneers with their crows and axes, breaking down the gates and forcing a passage. This was attended with some difficulty, and gave the enemy time for preparation. They raised their war-whoop, and resisted most manfully, fighting with spears, sabres, and muskets. They had also a few brass pieces mounted in the fort, but they managed them with so little skill as to produce no effect, for the balls uniformly whizzed over the heads of our men. The resistance of the natives was in vain. The fort was stormed and soon carried; not, however, till almost every individual in it was slain. To'onkou N'Yamat, usually called Po Mahomet, a chief of much distinction among the people, who had been principally concerned in the piratical act of taking the *Friendship,* lost his life at this fort. The mother of Chadoolah, another rajah, was also slain here. Another woman met her death at this fort, but her rank was not ascertained; she fought with the spirit of a desperado.

The sword of war should ever distinguish between armed and unarmed opponents, but if women openly jeopardize their lives in the forefront of battle, can it be expected that they will escape unharmed? A seaman had just scaled one of the ramparts when he was severely wounded by a blow received from a weapon in her hands. But her own life paid the forfeit of her daring, for she was immediately transfixed by a bayonet in the hands of the individual whom she had so severely injured. The seaman's head was wounded by a javelin, his thumb nearly cut off by a sabre, and a ball was shot through his hat. Had it not been for his fortitude and activity, he must inevitably have lost his life.

Lieutenants Edson and Terret, accompanied by a corps of marines, proceeded onward to the rear of the town, without commencing any act of hostility, till they arrived within the neighborhood of the fort which they had been ordered to assail. A bold attack was made upon the fort, and after a spirited resistance on the part of the enemy, it surrendered. Both officers and marines here narrowly escaped with their lives. One 'of the natives in the fort had trained his piece in such a manner as to rake their whole body, when he was shot down by a marine, while in the very act of applying a match to it. The cannon was afterwards found to have been filled with bullets. This fort, like the former, was environed with thick jungle, and great difficulty had been experienced in entering it. But for their crowbars and axes, the men could not have succeeded. A fire was opened near this fort from a neighboring thicket, upon the marines, by a party of the natives in ambush. It is probable that this was the spot where the unfortunate Brown lost his life. In the vicinity of this fort, Lieutenant Edson found several women and children greatly terrified, and it was with difficulty that he could pacify them. They were carefully conducted to a place of safety, where they remained till the close of the action, when they were humanely released.

The engagement had now become general, and the alarm universal. Men, women, and children were seen flying in every direction, carrying the few articles they were able to seize in the moment of peril, and some of the men were cut down in their flight. Several of the enemy's prows, filled with people, were severely raked by a brisk fire from the 6-pounder, as they were sailing up the river to the south of the town, and numbers of the natives were killed. One of these prows was taken by a party of men belonging to a chief by the name of Po Adam, who resides at Pulo Kio (woody island) on the opposite side of the river. This was the same prow that had been taken from him, a year previous to our arrival, by order of the King of Acheen. Adam is a true friend to the Americans.

A third fort was attacked under the command of Lieutenant Shubrick, assisted by Lieutenant Ingersoll and his division of men, together with acting Sailing-master Totten, in charge of a 6-pounder. Lieutenant Pinkham, being from some cause unable to find the fort he was directed to attack, joined them with his detachment; and the marines, not long after, united in like manner with the main body of the forces. This fort proved the most formidable. It was the largest and the strongest fortified, and the co-operation of the several divisions was ultimately required for its reduction; but so spirited was the fire poured into it by our troops that it was soon forced to yield; and the next moment, the American colors were seen triumphantly waving over its battlements. The greater part of the town was reduced to ashes. The bazaar, the principal place of merchandise, and most of the private dwellings were consumed by fire. The triumph had now been completed over the Malays; ample satisfaction had been taken for their outrages committed upon our countrymen, and the bugle sounded the return of the ship's forces; and the embarkation soon after was effected. The action had continued about two hours and a half, and was gallantly sustained by both officers and men from its commencement to its close.[5]

The loss of the Americans in this their first engagement in the Orient was two killed and 11 wounded, among the latter being Lieutenant Edson and Midshipman J. W. Taylor. Shubrick estimated that the enemy lost at least 150 men killed. Po Mahomet, the principal rajah concerned in the capture of the *Friendship,* was among the dead. Rajah Po Quallan fled at the beginning of the fight and two other rajahs were absent from the town. Most of the captured cannon were spiked and thrown over the parapets. One pair of colors, 26 stands of arms, and one brass field-piece were captured. Among the spoils of war were a Chinese gong, a Koran, and several pieces of rich gold cloth. Many of the men returned laden with rajah's scarfs and shawls, creeses richly hilted and with gold scabbards, gold and silver chuman boxes, pieces of money, ear-rings, finger-rings, anklets, bracelets, and other ornaments. Some of the sailors promised themselves a rich repast upon chickens and ducks, but going on board sooner than they expected they were compelled to leave the captured fowls on shore.

Soon after the return of the landing party, Downes stood towards the town and fired several broadsides into a fort that had been inaccessible to Shubrick, causing it to display a white flag. He next hoisted a white flag on board the *Potomac* as a signal that hostilities had been concluded. Then getting under way he sailed to the neighboring port of Soo-soo where he remained a few days. While lying there he received a flag of truce from Quallah Battoo, the bearer of which informed him that many of the inhabitants had been killed and all their property destroyed. He begged the commodore to grant them peace. Downes replied that he was now satisfied and that peace was granted, but that if they again committed piracy and murder upon American citi-

[5] Warriner, Francis. Cruise of the United States Frigate *Potomac,* 87-91.

zens other ships of war would be sent to inflict further punishment. Alarmed at the fate that had befallen Quallah Battoo, the
rajahs of some of the neighboring towns sent delegations to
Downes to declare their friendship for him, and to present him
with propitiatory gifts of fruits and vegetables. The summary
vengeance inflicted by the *Potomac* was long remembered by the
natives, and had a most salutary effect. At home Downes was
criticised by some of the newspapers for the severity of the chastisement administered to the Quallah Battooans, but not by President Jackson, who approved the course pursued by him.

On February 18 the *Potomac* sailed from Soo-soo for Pan-
goriang in Bantam Bay on the coast of Java, where a supply of
wood and water was obtained. Thence she went to Batavia, from
which place Downes proceeded to Buitenzorg to call upon the
governor of Java. On the passage to Macao the commodore's
secretary died of consumption and was buried at sea. It is worthy
of remark as illustrative of the generosity of sailors that the
officers and crew of the *Potomac* contributed more than $2000
for the support of the children of the dead man. From Macao
some of the officers made an excursion to Canton. Early in June
the *Potomac* sailed for the Pacific Station by way of the Sandwich Islands. She finally arrived home in May, 1834, having
circumnavigated the globe from west to east, the first American
ship of war to accomplish that feat.

VII

Diplomatic Missions to China, Siam, and Muscat, *1832-1837*[6]

To make sure that satisfaction would be obtained for the outrage committed on the *Friendship,* the Secretary of the Navy in January, 1832, decided to send a little fleet composed of the sloop of war *Peacock,* Master-Commandant David Geisinger, and the schooner *Boxer,* Lieutenant W. F. Shields, to Quallah Battoo to carry out Commodore Downes's orders in case that officer should fail to do so. From Quallah Battoo, Geisinger was to proceed to Macao and protect our commerce in Chinese waters. On his return voyage he was to visit certain Asiatic and African ports and afford every facility (quoting the words of the Secretary of the Navy) "to Mr. Roberts, the gentleman who acts in the capacity of clerk to the commander of the *Peacock,* to enable him to carry into effect and success his instructions from the State Department." As the chief events of Geisinger's cruise are connected with Roberts's mission a brief account of its origin may be here presented.

Edmund Roberts was a prosperous merchant and ship owner of Portsmouth, New Hampshire. His commercial interests led

---

[6] The principal sources of information used in writing this chapter are Captains' Letters, December, 1835, 1; August, 1836, 2; Commanders' Letters, U. S. Navy Department Archives, October, 1832, 9; July-December, 1833, 1; January-June, 1834, 108; Letters to Officers of Ships of War, XX, 242, 244; XXI, 421, 507; Roberts, Edmund, Embassy to the Eastern Courts, 5-6, 171-257, 351-363; Foster, J. W., American Diplomacy in the Orient, 45-54; Ruschenberger, W. S. W., A Voyage Round the World, 89-94, 319-320, 340-344.

him to visit the Orient and to study the needs and possibilities of American trade in that part of the globe. Convinced that the establishment of commercial treaties with certain Eastern rulers would prove highly beneficial to his countrymen, he wrote to Levi Woodbury, one of the New Hampshire senators at Washington detailing the neglected state of our trade and showing that the favors granted to Great Britain in the Orient gave that country an advantage over our own. Soon after Woodbury became Secretary of the Navy, Roberts was appointed a special envoy of the State Department and clerk to the commander of the *Peacock,* and was authorized to negotiate treaties with the courts of Cochin China, Siam, and Muscat, placing our commerce on an equality with that of the most favored nations. He was also to visit Japan if he found " the prospect favorable."

David Geisinger, the commander of the *Peacock,* entered the navy as a midshipman in 1809, and became a lieutenant in 1814, a master commandant in 1829, and a captain in 1834. He was one of the officers of the *Wasp* during her notable cruise off the English coast in 1814, and had the good fortune to be sent home in command of the prize *Atalanta,* thus escaping the fate of his shipmates who were lost with their vessel at sea.

In March, 1832, the *Peacock* sailed from Boston for Rio Janeiro, where she expected the *Boxer* to join her. Disappointed in her expectations, she, on June 25, went to sea without her consort, and two months later came to anchor in the Bay of Bencoolen on the west coast of Sumatra. Learning here of the destruction of Quallah Battoo by Commodore Downes, she proceeded to Lintin by way of Manila. The success of Downes and the satisfactory state of our commerce with China left Geisinger free to pursue the remaining objects of his cruise. Having received on board Mr. John R. Morrison, a son of Dr. Robert Morrison, who was to act as interpreter, translator, and private secretary to the envoy, he sailed from Lintin for Turan Bay, on the east coast of Cochin China, regarded as the best place from which to communicate with Hué, the capital of that country, 50 miles distant. Unfortunately he was prevented from entering the bay by contrary winds and a strong current setting to the eastward. He, therefore, bore away for the port of Vunglam, where he arrived on January 6, 1833, and where he remained more than a month.

From Vunglam, Roberts entered into communication with some minor officials of the Cochin China government, with whom he held numerous parleys and conferences, they at times coming on board and he, accompanied with Geisinger, going ashore. As a preliminary to the opening of negotiations, the officials insisted upon many formalities, more or less insulting to the Americans, to all of which Roberts refused to accede. They asked to see President Jackson's letter to the Emperor, they found fault with Morrison's translation of it, and they objected to the rank of the envoy. On this latter point Roberts succeeded in satisfying them by adding to his title of " special envoy from the United States and a citizen of Portsmouth, New Hampshire," the names of the counties of his State and several of its towns, thereby giving his name a most distinguished and formidable appearance. The principal official remarked that the envoy had more titles than any prince of the empire. Roberts's immediate object was to obtain permission to visit the Emperor or to enter into communication with him and his chief minister. Failing in this, he abandoned his mission to Cochin China.

From Vunglam the *Peacock* sailed for the Gulf of Siam and after a 10 days' voyage arrived at the bar of the Menam River. Communication was at once opened with the King of Siam, who courteously sent three boats to convey the American embassy to Bangkok, the Siamese capital. A party consisting of Geisinger, Roberts, Morrison, and several officers, were thus conveyed to Bangkok, where on their arrival they found a house especially prepared for their accommodation by the king, who also provided them with a cook, a purveyor, servants, and a superintendent, and feasted and entertained them in a royal manner throughout their stay. As the king was quite willing to treat with the United States, Roberts and the Siamese minister of foreign affairs at once began negotiations and on March 20 completed their labors by signing a treaty of amity and commerce—the first diplomatic instrument executed by the United States and an Asiatic power. It fixed the duties to be paid by American merchantmen on entering Siamese ports, abolished certain barbarous penalties for debts, and provided for the friendly treatment of shipwrecked American sailors.

Shortly before the embassy returned to the *Peacock,* it paid a visit to the king, who received it in accordance with the manners and customs of his court. Of this reception Roberts has left us the following account:

We entered at length the vestibule through a line of soldiers, and passed to the right of a Chinese screen of painted glass, into the presence of His Majesty. There lay prostrate, or rather on all fours resting on their knees and elbows, with hands united and head bowed low, all the princes and nobility of the land; it was an impressive but an abasing sight, such as no freeman could look on with any other feelings than those of indignation and disgust. We halted in front of the presents which were delivered the day previous, being piles of silks, rich fillagreed silver baskets, elegant gold watches studded with large pearls; they were well disposed to make a show. Having gone through the first ceremony of bowing, we sat down on a carpet; on our being seated the prostrate slaves around us (being the great men of the land) bowed simultaneously three times to the ground, in a slow solemn manner, and we joined in the ceremony as had been previously agreed upon. The king was seated under a canopy, in the Asiatic style, on a cushion of red silk velvet, on the lower and more advanced of the two thrones, which occupied the upper end of the apartment; this was a square seat raised some half dozen feet from the floor. Everything was blazing in gold in and about the two thrones; the larger and unoccupied one was of an hexagonal shape, and resembled a church pulpit, so that the king's person when seated in it, can be visible only through the open spaces, in the form of Gothic windows, about four feet in height by one and a half and two in width. One of these windows is in front, and one on each side of the throne. A pair of curtains of gold cloth formed a partition between him and several individuals of the royal family, who lay crouching just without, on separate carpets, leaving a wide open space between the throne and the two interpreters, who were midway of the hall. Before the curtain and on either side, were eight or ten umbrellas of various sizes; these consist of a series of canopies of eight or ten tiers, decreasing in size upward.

His Majesty is a very stout, fleshy man, apparently about 45 years of age, of a pleasing countenance. He was dressed in a cloth of gold tissue around the waist, while a mantle was thrown gracefully over the left shoulder. Four noblemen's sons were seated at the base of the throne, at the rear and sides, having long-handled pear-shaped fans, richly gilt, which they kept in constant motion. A few questions were addressed by the king in an audible voice; they were repeated in a lower tone by the phaya phiphat, or second praklang, to the phaya churat, or chief of the Chuliahs, by whom they were whispered to the captain of the port, who interpreted them to us in the same low tone—the answers were returned through the same channels by us—inquiring, in the first place, as to the health of the President and all the great men in our country; our own healths; those of the officers and crew; how long we had been from America; where we had been, and whence bound; desiring me to acquaint the praklang with all my wants, that they might be supplied, etc. The curtain was now drawn and His Majesty disappeared; the court made three solemn kotows, and we our three salams, and then retired.[7]

[7] Roberts, Edmund. Embassy to the Eastern Courts, 256-257.

From Siam the *Peacock* went to Singapore to land Morrison and to obtain supplies, and thence to Batavia, where she was joined by the *Boxer*. After calling at Anjer, the two ships sailed for Mocha, Arabia, in the Red Sea, where they arrived on August 31. Of their visit to this port and their subsequent movements, Captain Geisinger wrote as follows:

I found the place in possession of a Turkish rebel chieftain, named Turkie ben Almas, from Grand Cairo. I was informed he had taken and held this and other places on the eastern side of the Red Sea in the name of the Grand Seignor, but his authority for so doing was not yet recognized by his master. He was formerly an officer in the service of the Pacha of Egypt, and it is quite a doubtful case yet whether he has taken possession of the country for the Sublime Porte, for the Pacha of Egypt or for himself. He evinced a very friendly disposition towards us and the American flag, and expressed high gratification in seeing two American vessels of war in the port, being the first, he was told, that were ever in the Red Sea. In fact it was supposed by the people of Mocha that there were no vessels of that description belonging to our country, or else they would have occasionally visited this and other neighboring places for the protection of our extensive commerce. Our stay at this place was necessarily very limited owing to the near expiration of the southwest monsoon, and, therefore, on the evening of the first of September we sailed for Muscat, the principal place of destination in these seas, and on the 18th of the same month both vessels anchored in the cove of Muscat.

The most friendly disposition was manifested by the Sultan and his officers during our stay, and supplies of wood, water, etc., were furnished gratuitously. We found him very intelligent and affable and greatly beloved by his subjects. Without doubt full reliance may be placed in his faithfully fulfilling his engagements. He now owns eight ships of war, carrying 22 to 74 guns, and 57 sail of vessels (variously rigged) carrying from four to 18 guns—with a very extensive commerce. The Sultan did us the honor to visit the *Peacock* and was received with the highest honors we were capable of bestowing. He examined every part of the ship and expressed himself in strong terms of admiration at what he considered her fine condition, etc. The Sultan having made several voyages in his own ships of war to his possessions in Africa and elsewhere, is considered to be a good judge of everything relating to naval affairs.[8]

The Sultan of Muscat was a powerful prince who ruled over a large territory extending from the Persian Gulf to the southern limits of Zanzibar. Our merchantmen carried on a considerable trade with his people, the increase and improvement of which was one of the objects of Roberts's embassy. On the day after the arrival of the two ships, Roberts, Geisinger, and Lieutenant Shields had an audience with the Sultan and he readily consented to enter into a treaty with the United States, willingly grant-

[8] Masters' Letters, January-June, 1834, 108.

ing larger concessions than our envoy asked for. By the terms of the treaty signed on September 21, our commerce with his dominions was placed on the same footing as that of the most favored nations, and he promised to support our shipwrecked sailors at his own expense until they found an opportunity to return home.

From Muscat the *Peacock* and *Boxer* sailed for Rio Janeiro, touching on their way at Mozambique and the Cape of Good Hope. As they were to remain on the Brazil Station, Roberts took passage for the United States on the sloop of war *Lexington,* arriving at Boston on April 24, 1834. His treaties with Siam and Muscat were ratified by the President and Senate on June 30, and he was shortly thereafter commissioned to return to those countries and exchange ratifications. He also received orders to make another attempt to negotiate with Cochin China, and to visit Japan and enter into treaty with the ruler of that nation.

To add dignity to the new embassy a little squadron, under the command of a commodore, was placed at the service of the envoy. It consisted of the sloop of war *Peacock,* Commander C. K. Stribling, and the schooner *Enterprise,* Lieutenant A. S. Campbell, both under the command of Commodore E. P. Kennedy, who was authorized by the Department to hoist his broad pennant on board his flagship. Kennedy thus gained the distinction of being the first commander of the "East India squadron." He entered the navy as a midshipman in 1805, and after serving in various stations as a subordinate officer attained the rank of captain in 1828. He died in 1844 while in command of the line of battle ship *Pennsylvania.*

On July 12, 1835, Kennedy sailed with his squadron from Rio Janeiro for Muscat. Three days out of port the *Enterprise,* proving to be a dull sailer, was given orders to part company with the flagship and pursue her own course to the Indian Ocean. The *Peacock* arrived at Zanzibar on September 2. For the stirring events of her cruise during the next few weeks, Kennedy's narrative is the best authority:

The *Enterprise* not having arrived, we sailed from Zanzibar on the 8th September for Muscat; and on the 21st, about two hours after midnight, an almost fatal accident befell the *Peacock* by being stranded near the island of Mazeira, on the desolate coast of Arabia. At meridian on the day previous the ship was found by the chronometers, etc., to be 72 miles to the eastward of that island; and it was intended to preserve that distance from the coast until we should come into the latitude of Cape Ras al

Had. But to the violent and uncertain currents on that coast (of which we were ignorant until after the accident), also to the fact that the island is placed on the charts upwards of 30 miles too far to the westward (which has been ascertained by the survey now prosecuting on that coast by order of the British government) must be attributed our misfortune.

After several ineffectual attempts to heave the ship off into deeper water (which failed owing to the anchors breaking and coming home), we became fearful she would be destroyed by the first gale, when no succor could be had short of Muscat, a distance of upwards of 400 miles. The boats, being incapable of saving one-third of the crew, were constantly beset, too, by numerous piratical vessels, who attempted in a most audacious manner to cut off the launch and cutters when carrying out anchors—using also every stratagem to plunder our raft of provisions, etc., and while their number was hourly augmented they clearly manifested the purpose of destroying us and making prize of the ship so soon as they were in sufficient force. Placed in this perilous situation, with very slight hopes of saving the ship, having on board only a small supply of water, in a climate where the sun burns with an intensity which can scarcely be surpassed, I could only look to Muscat for assistance. Being unable to spare either of the large boats, on which rested our only hope of saving the ship and crew, and it being very inconvenient to send a lieutenant on that service, Mr. Roberts, our envoy to Asia, with a promptness and fearlessness which mark all his movements, most kindly volunteered his services to proceed on this most dangerous expedition in an open boat 20 feet in length amidst numerous piratical craft and a boisterous sea, accompanied by Passed Midshipman Wm. R. Taylor and six men. They arrived safely at Muscat in 101 hours, having been pursued by pirates and more than once nearly lost owing to the boat filling with water.

As soon as the situation was made known to the Sultan by Mr. Roberts (with whom he was previously well acquainted) the former forthwith ordered the *Sultana*, a new sloop of war, to be prepared by noon of the following day to proceed to the Gulf of Mazeira with a supply of water and provisions. A courier was likewise dispatched to the Governor of Zoar, a large town near Ras al Had, with orders for him to proceed immediately with six large dows, carring 300 soldiers and a quantity of supplies, to protect the ship and crew until the arrival of the *Sultana*. Having determined to omit no measure which could benefit us, he likewise ordered 350 Bedouins to proceed overland for the protection of the crew in case it became necessary to seek shelter on that most wretched coast. Within one hour and three-quarters from the time of Mr. Roberts's arrival, the ship was preparing for sea, the courier many miles on his way to Zoar, and the Bedouins were in readiness to mount their camels. The *Sultana* sailed at the appointed time, and the next morning we fell in with her about 50 miles from Muscat.

Two days after the boat left us, having lightened the ship by starting three-fourths of our water, everything in the spirit-room, and throwing overboard one-half of our guns, a large quantity of shot, two chain and one hemp cable, rafting sundry barrels of provisions, naval stores and our spare spars (which were finally lost), and striking everything from aloft, we were most fortunately enabled by the great and unceasing efforts and perseverance of the officers and crew, who conducted themselves perfectly to my satisfaction, to heave the ship into deep water, and then to reach Muscat, although in a very leaky condition.

During our stay at Muscat, which was no longer than necessary to complete the business with which Mr. Roberts was entrusted by the Department of State, the Sultan supplied us with large quantities of provisions, vegetables, and fruit, and paid us such personal attention as laid us all under obligations that can never be forgotten. The good Sultan, being still unwearied in his efforts to serve our country through us, dispatched several large boats to Mazeira and saved the 11 pieces of lost cannon. They were carried to Muscat laden on board a baghelo and sent to this place [Bombay], where they have arrived after others had been purchased, but which have been returned to the government from whom they were received. I have made suitable acknowledgement for his truly friendly and unsurpassed promptness in every measure that could benefit us, or contributed to our personal comfort.[9]

On September 30 the ratified treaty was exchanged with the Sultan, and 10 days later Roberts and Kennedy took final leave of that generous ruler. The *Peacock* proceeded to Siam by way of Bombay, Colombo, and Batavia. At Bombay, where she was thoroughly repaired, facilities for such work being freely offered by the officers of the British East India Company, she met the *Enterprise,* and thence the two vessels sailed in company, being the first American warships to visit British India. Late in March, 1836, they arrived at the mouth of the river Menam, whence Roberts, Kennedy, and several officers went to Bangkok, where they were most courteously received by the Siamese government. The exchange of ratifications was attended with much pomp and ceremony. The delivery of the treaty to the officers appointed to receive it is thus described by the surgeon of the *Peacock,* who witnessed the proceeding:

Mr. Roberts took the treaty in his hand, and, after holding it up above his head in token of respect, delivered it to a Siamese officer, the secretary of the P'hra Klang. He also held it above his head, and then shaded by a royal chat (a large white silk umbrella) borne by a slave, passed it into the boat, where it was received upon an ornamental stand, and after covering it with a cone of gilt paper, it was placed beneath the canopy. At this moment our band ceased, and that of the Siamese began to play.[10]

The date of the exchange of ratifications was April 14, 1836. Two days before this the commodore was compelled by illness to return to his ship, and soon after the ceremony at Bangkok,

[9] Captains' Letters, December, 1835, 1.

[10] Ruschenberger, W. S. W. A Voyage Round the World, 319-320.

Roberts and the rest of the party came on board, all of them un-well and some of them seriously sick, with cholera and dysentery. The squadron next proceeded to Turan Bay, where it remained eight days, at the end of which time, Roberts, having tried in vain to open negotiations with the Emperor of Cochin China and being still sick, abandoned his mission to that country. On May 22 the squadron arrived at Macao, with 61 men sick with cholera and dysentery. Provision for the invalids was made at a tem-porary hospital on shore, where most of them rapidly recovered. Lieutenant Campbell and Mr. Roberts, however, died, early in June, and they were buried at Macao. The officers of the squadron erected a monument to the memory of Campbell, and the American merchants residing in China contributed the money for a similar memorial to Roberts—the first American diplomat in the Far East.

The visit to Japan was now abandoned. On June 23, 1836, Kennedy sailed from Macao for home by way of the Bonin Islands, Sandwich Islands, and the west coast of North and South America. He arrived at Hampton Roads on October 27, 1837, having been at sea 524 days, and having sailed 54,285 miles.

VIII

The *Vincennes* in the Western Pacific, *1835-1836*[11]

In the spring of 1834 Secretary of the Navy Levi Woodbury ordered Commodore Alexander Wadsworth, commander of the Pacific squadron, to dispatch one of the sloops of war under his command on a cruise to the Feejee and Pellew Islands, China, and Sumatra. The sloop selected by Wadsworth was the *Vincennes,* Commander John H. Aulick, which vessel, it is recollected, made her first voyage to the Orient in 1829-1830, under the command of Captain Finch.

Aulick entered the navy as a midshipman in 1809, and was promoted to a lieutenantcy in 1814 and a captaincy in 1841. He saw important service in both the War of 1812 and the Mexican War. In the former conflict he served for a time as a junior officer on board the *Enterprise,* displaying much gallantry in that vessel's engagement with the British brig *Boxer.* His work as commander-in-chief of the East India squadron in 1852-1853 will be described in a succeeding chapter.

Aulick's executive officer on the *Vincennes* was Lieutenant John A. Carr. Two of his junior lieutenants were Theodorus Bailey and Samuel P. Lee (a grandson of the Revolutionary statesman, Richard Henry Lee), both of whom fought bravely in the Civil War, and became rear-admirals. Aulick's orders directed him to proceed to the Feejee and Pellew Islands and receive on board his ship any American whalemen or sailors

---

[11] The chief sources of information for this chapter are Letters to Officers of Ships of War, XX, 454; XXI, 66; Masters' Letters, January-June, 1836, 5, 54; Niles' Register, XLIV, 421.

desirous of returning home, to call at Macao and Quallah Battoo for the protection of our commerce, and to make enquiries at all the places visited by him respecting the condition of our trade and the treatment of our citizens. Another particular object of his cruise was the rescuing of the survivors of the New Bedford ship *Mentor,* Captain Edward C. Barnard, which was wrecked on one of the Pellew Islands in May, 1832, situated some 500 miles eastward of the Philippines. About six months after the disaster Barnard and several of his men, accompanied by three natives, went to sea in a whaleboat and a canoe, hoping to reach the Dutch East Indies. The canoe was sunk in a squall and the whaleboat was captured by the natives of Lord North's Island— a small island lying in the neighborhood of the Moluccas. Here in February, 1833, the captain and one of his men were rescued by the Spanish ship *Sabina,* which carried them to Macao, the rest of the crew of the whaleboat being left behind.

Aulick's eventful cruise began with his leaving Callao on one of the last days of July, 1835, and ended with his arrival at Hampton Roads, a little more than 10 months later, on June 5, 1836. He crossed the Pacific in the latitude of South America instead of making a detour northward to the Sandwich Islands, the course followed by all our naval commanders preceding him. He was also the first to visit the island of Guam, our future possession. Soon after his return to the United States he prepared for the Secretary of the Navy a detailed account of his cruise, which is particularly significant for the information it contains respecting our whaling interests, and for the view it gives of the limited knowledge regarding Oceanica possessed by the civilized world in the first half of the nineteenth century. Aulick's report, in large part, was as follows:

Although my orders from the commodore, directing my return home by way of India, mentioned only the Feejee and Pellew Islands, as those which I was required to visit for specific purposes, the general object of my cruise being as matter of course the protection of our citizens and their interests wherever it might be in my power to afford it, I deemed it my duty, as well from this consideration as with a view to procure as often as possible those refreshments for my crew believed to be essential to the preservation of their health, to touch at such other places on or near my route, as are known to be frequented, for supplies, etc., by our numerous whalers and traders scattered over those seas.

Accordingly on taking my departure from the coast of Peru, I directed my course for the Washington Group, and after a short passage of 19 days, anchored in Massachusetts Bay, Island of Nooaheevah, on the 18th of August. Our reception by the natives was extremely cordial and friendly. The former visit of this ship, and Commodore Porter's long sojourn among them continue to be remembered, and I believe still exercise a favorable influence on their conduct generally towards all foreigners who visit them. They do not, however, appear to have made any progress towards civilization since the commodore left them, or to have risen in any respect above their character and condition at that time, as described in the journal of his cruise. Acts of treachery and savage violence are still occasionally committed on defenceless strangers, and it behooves all such to be constantly on their guard in their intercourse with them, on all parts of the island, but particularly at the Valley of the Typees. From the best information I could obtain there are on an average about 20 American whalers touch here in the course of the year. Water, wood, vegetables, and fruit are readily obtained here for trifles, but hogs are reserved expressly for the purpose of purchasing muskets and powder; so that I, not being disposed to trade in these articles, was scarcely able to procure one fresh mess for my crew during our stay. But on this point they do not always find their visitors so particular; and I was sorry to learn that, through means of our countrymen chiefly, they were already in possession of a considerable number of arms, and some ammunition.

We sailed thence on the 27th, taking with us two of four American seamen, whom we found there. The other two refused to leave the island. On the 5th September we arrived at Otaheita (Tahiti). This place is much resorted to by our whalers, who find it particularly convenient for refitting and procuring supplies. Some few traders also call here, and, in exchange for various articles of merchandise, get arrow root and cocoanut oil, of which, however, owing to the extreme indolence of the natives, but very small quantities are produced for exportation. No public records of any kind, as I was told, are kept by the islanders, nor could I learn from any source the number of American arrivals there annually; but from a memorandum kept by one of the missionary gentlemen, for about six months of the year 1832, it appears that during that period 42 vessels had anchored in Papeete Harbor alone, of which 29 were American, chiefly whalers. Two arrived while we were there, and several others appeared in the offing. Scarcely any depart without leaving some of their crew behind, either from desertion, sickness, or from their being literally turned adrift by the captains. On our arrival I was informed that there was not less than 20 American seamen lounging about the island in a destitute condition. I immediately caused it to be made known that I would give a passage to all who were desirous of returning to their native country; and the Queen Pomare, having expressed to me great anxiety to get rid of all foreigners of this description, I was induced to prolong my stay beyond my original intention in order that those who were at distant villages, might have time to avail themselves of my offer. Eleven got on board before we sailed, and were entered as supernumeraries for rations.

We left Tahiti on the 20th, with Queen Pomare and her family on board, she having requested a passage to the next island to the westward, laying directly in my route; and in the afternoon of the same day we landed her at Eimeo. Thence I pursued my course for the Friendly and

Feejee Islands, passing within sight of Whytootacke, one of the Hervey Group, and directly over the place (latitude 19° 7′ south, and longitude 171° 46′ west) assigned to an island on a list of new discoveries in my possession; but no signs of land were visible.

On the 1st of October we arrived at Port Refuge, Vavaoo [one of the Friendly Islands]. In this beautiful harbor we found, to our very agreeable surprise, six American whalers at anchor. Here they ride completely landlocked, secure from the dangers of stormy weather and entirely free from anxiety as to the conduct of the natives, who, though but a few years ago justly ranked among the most savage and treacherous of all the islanders, have now become, as I am well assured, through the persevering exertions of the worthy missionaries residing among them, as honest, amiable, and friendly as those of either the Sandwich or Society Islands. Our arrival was hailed with much satisfaction by the masters of the whalers, for some of whom it proved to be quite opportune. Most of them had been unsuccessful in whaling. Their men, discouraged and dissatisfied, had become insubordinate, and in one instance actually mutinous to such a degree, that at the request of the captain I took out the ringleaders and confined them in irons on board this ship, until by their, at least apparently, sincere penitence and promise of future good behavior, he was induced to receive them on board again. Two of the vessels had lost a number of their crews by desertion. Their deficiencies I was enabled to supply from our list of supernumeraries, to the satisfaction of all parties.

My principal object in touching at this place was to obtain information, if possible, relative to the navigation of the Feejees, of which I had neither chart nor description that could be of the least service to me as a guide in sailing among them. The account I now received from the missionary residents and native chiefs of both this and of the Feejees (several of the latter being here on a visit), as well as from the captains of the whalers, two of whom had been recently cruising in sight of them, fully confirmed what I had been told at Tahiti and elsewhere, namely: that the group consists of more than a hundred islands, scattered over a space of a thousand miles in circumference; that each island is separately encircled by a reef, and the whole group interspersed with numerous and extensive coral reefs and shoals; that not more than two or three places of anchorage are known, and those could only be reached by intricate passages through the reefs; in short that it was believed to be the most dangerous navigation in the world, and ought not to be attempted by a heavy ship like the *Vincennes,* at least without a small vessel in company to lead the way and examine the ground ahead. The captain of a small English trader that had been wrecked there a few years ago, in a note addressed to me on this subject uses the following language: "I have no hesitation to say it is perhaps the worst navigation in the world; in fact it makes me shudder to think on the narrow escapes I had before losing my vessel, and what I suffered after. Be cautious and do not venture over the ground at night that you have not gone over in the day."

These accounts altogether presented certainly a discouraging picture. Nevertheless had my orders been peremptory on this point, nothing should have prevented at least an effort on my part to comply with them, but such was not the case. They required only that I should "visit the Feejee and Pellew Islands, if practicable without great delay or danger"; thus leaving it at my own discretion and on my own responsibility to act as I might judge proper, of course after obtaining the best information I could on the subject. From the information obtained as above stated, it was evidently not practicable without great danger, and, considering the extent of the group and the great number of islands composing it, it was equally evident to my mind that to pay them such a visit as would be likely to produce good effects, if at all practicable, could not be done without greater delay than our limited quantity of provisions and the other duties yet to be performed before reaching China would warrant. To have simply shown the ship off the islands, without getting near enough to satisfy the natives of our power to act efficiently against them, if disposed to do so, would only have had a tendency to confirm them in the security of their position, and probably render them still more audacious and dangerous to defenceless traders than they already are. Under all considerations then, I could hardly have felt myself justified in attempting the prosecution of that part of my orders, even had no other motive for its relinquishment existed. But I had other strong inducements for the course I determined to pursue, and which course I hope may meet the approbation of the Department.

I had just learnt from Captain Toby, commander of one of the whalers, that about a year before that time two of the boats of the American whaler *Wm. Penn* had been cut off, and part of their crews murdered by the natives of Oteewhy, or Savie, one of the Navigators Islands. Toby had been there since, had purchased from the chiefs one of the boats, and ransomed some of the men, one of whom made the statement herewith enclosed and numbered "1," from which it appears that no provocation was given by the people of the boats, but that the sole motive for the diabolical outrage was plunder. In addition to this I was informed by several of these captains that an American ship had been seen ashore on one of the Caroline Islands, but a few months before that time. They did not recollect the name of the island, but said they got their information from an American residing at Rotumah, from whom I would be able to obtain the particulars.

Situated, as I now found myself, within three days' sail of Oteewhy, and at no great distance from the Carolines, I felt it incumbent upon me to proceed immediately and endeavor in the first place to punish the wretches who had cut off the boats and rescue the remaining captives; and, when that affair was settled, to hasten to the relief of the ship on shore. Accordingly, having obtained a particular description of the place and of the chief who led the murderous gang, I left Fort Refuge on the 7th in company with all our whalers, and on the 9th had the Navigators in view. The next day being off Oteewhy, and, having masked our ports and otherwise disguised the ship so as to give her as much as possible the appearance of a whaler, we stood close in upon the southwest side of the island where the outrage had been committed; and, as I anticipated, we soon had a canoe alongside, on board which besides eight natives were two Englishmen, who had resided some years on the island and spoke the language fluently. These I immediately pressed into service to act as guides. The natives were brought on board, and the canoe hoisted up to prevent escape. Unfortunately the day was too far gone to admit of our landing an expedition before night, and the landing place was said to be too difficult and dangerous to be attempted in the dark. There being no anchorage here, we stood off and on during the night, and the next morning I despatched Lieutenant Carr with 80 marines and musketeers; and gave him orders to endeavor to capture the chief and as many of his followers as he could, and bring them on board the ship uninjured if possible, to bring off any arms he might find and to set fire to the town and destroy it. In the evening Mr. Carr returned and reported that he landed his party without opposition. He found the town deserted, and destroyed it as directed, with whatever the houses contained. The natives had fled to the mountains, where they were so thoroughly sheltered by the rocks and underwood that it was not thought advisable to pursue them.

Oteewhy is an island of perhaps 150 miles in circumference, and not under the authority of a single chief, but is divided into several sections, each of which has its separate and independent chief. Aware of this fact, I had charged Mr. Carr to avoid with the utmost care a collision with the neighboring tribes, who the guides told us had no concern in the atrocious act, to endeavor to open a friendly intercourse with some of them and explain the reasons of our descent upon their island, and assure them it was our wish to punish only the guilty. In this he was perfectly successful. A friendly chief, with some of his people, accompanied him on board, and readily admitted to me the justice of the chastisement inflicted on his neighbor, who he said was a very bad man, and he seemed to regret that we had not been able to capture him. Although this expedition did not succeed to the full extent of my wishes, still the display of an armed force upon their shore, to which they did not dare offer resistance, and the destruction of their town and considerable other property, will, I am persuaded, be long remembered by them, and I trust with a good effect on their conduct towards future visitors. The only man (a Sandwich Islander) of the captured boats' crews, that was then on the island, contrived to get off to us, and is now on board this ship. The other boat had been sold to an English whaler but a few weeks before we arrived.

On the 13th we left the Navigators for Rotumah, taking Wallis Island (a favorite refreshing place of the whalers) in our route, and arrived there on the following day. This island is surrounded by a coral reef, within which there is a good harbor. The entrance, however, though deep, is so very narrow that I did not think it prudent to attempt it. We lay off and on two days, during which time we procured some water and a quantity of vegetables and fruit. Two American seamen, who had been left there by whalers, were at their request received on board for a passage home. On the 18th we arrived at Rotumah Island, also much frequented by whalers. One came in at the moment of our anchoring. Much to my regret I was not able to get any satisfactory information here relative to the vessel said to be ashore on one of the Carolines. The man to whom I had been referred perfectly recollected that an English brig had touched at Rotumah a few months before and reported having seen a bright-sided ship ashore on one of those islands, but the name and situation of the place he had entirely forgotten. I was, therefore, compelled to abandon all idea of affording her relief. The anchorage at this island being unsafe, I delayed only long enough to fill up our empty water-tanks.

It was my intention on leaving Rotumah to have held a course as nearly as possible direct for the Pellew Islands, which would have led us through a part of the ocean as yet but little known, and where I was in hopes I might be fortunate enough to make some new discovery. But to my great disappointment we very soon encountered strong westerly winds, which compelled us to stand to the northward, until in spite of ourselves we were carried into the midst of the great chain of the Caroline Islands, in longitude 167° E. We then had for a number of days a continuation of squally and thick weather, limiting our view of the horizon to so narrow a space, that it became necessary at times, as matter of prudence, to heave to even in the day time, lest we should run upon some one of the numerous islands or shoals, with which that part of the ocean is known to abound. In this situation, and with no time to spare, I thought it advisable to abandon all further attempt to get to the westward in a south latitude. Accordingly we continued on a northern course to gain the strength of the N. E. trade.

In crossing the parallel of the Carolines frequent indications of the vicinity of land were seen, such as green branches of trees and various kinds of land birds; and by our reckoning we must have passed very near several islands, if they were correctly laid down on the charts. We, however, got sight of only one group, consiting of a number of small, low islands and reefs, called " Brown's Range," in latitude 11° 30' N. and longitude 162° 30' E. It is said these islands were not inhabited when discovered in 1798. That they now are, there can be little doubt, as we saw a large canoe under sail near the land, and I regretted that the lateness of the hour, it being near night, prevented our communicating with her.

On the 19th November we passed between Rota and Guam (of the Marians) and hove to off Port Apra [Guam] where I had intended tc anchor for a day or two, but not liking the appearance of the bar and harbor, I delayed only long enough to get off some fruit and vegetables, after which we continued our route for the Pellew Islands, and on the 26th arrived in sight of them. As this whole group is well known to be almost entirely surrounded by dangerous reefs, and as I had no chart or plan upon which the dangers are described or the anchorage pointed out, prudence required that we should approach them with the greatest caution, and it was not until the 29th that, with one of the principal Rupacks on board as pilot, and an English sailor, who had been many years on the islands, as interpreter, we got to anchor in an open roadstead about eight miles from Corror. We soon received a visit from the king of that island, and were informed that two of the unfortunate *Mentor's* crew were still detained by the King of Baubelthonap, at a place called Arracolon, about 30 miles distant from our anchorage. We also learnt the following particulars on the subject:

When Captain Bernard left these islands after the loss of his ship in 1832, he promised the King of Baubelthonap, into whose hands he had fallen, to return as soon as possible with a certain number of muskets and other articles, which were to be given him as compensation for the maintenance of himself and crew while there, and the aid afforded them in getting away. As security for the faithful execution of this promise, three of his crew were detained by the king, and an equal number of the natives sent with him. At the period of our arrival they knew nothing of the disaster that had befallen the captain and his companions at North Island, and were anxiously looking out for his return. In the meantime one of the men had made his escape in a passing vessel, in consequence of which the other two were the more strictly guarded, and I was assured by the King of Corror (and have since learnt from the men themselves that such was really the fact) that the chiefs had determined to put them to death rather than suffer them to escape, or give them up until the muskets, etc., were paid, and their own people brought back. Under these circumstances it was not to be expected that they would be peaceably surrendered on my demanding them, particularly as it was well known that the ship could not approach nearer than to within 25 miles of Arracolon, on account of the extensive reefs; and to attempt their rescue by means of a boat expedition would by exasperating the savages undoubtedly put their lives in great peril. This course was, therefore, only to be resorted to as a last alternative. It being already my determination in any event to go to North's Island for the purpose of taking off any that might yet remain of those left there by Captain Bernard, I thought it best to proceed to that place at once, and if possible get off the Pellew-men also, and return to these islands, when I had no doubt our men on Baubelthonap would be readily liberated in exchange for theirs in our hands and thus all difficulty be amicably settled.

On the 9th December, six days from the Pellews, we arrived at North's Island, a low, level, green speck upon the ocean, not above a league in circumference, nor elevated probably more than 20 feet at its highest point, above the surface of the sea. Surrounded by a reef and thickly covered nearly to the water's edge with scarcely anything other than cocoanut trees, on the fruit of which a population of at least 400 human beings depend almost exclusively for both food and drink. We were quickly boarded by a number of canoes, in one of which came one of the Pellew chiefs, from whom we learnt the melancholy fate of the greater portion of his late companions. Of the nine men remaining after the escape of Captain Bernard in 1833, he was now the only survivor on the island. His two countrymen and four of the white men died literally from a want of proper and sufficient sustenance. The other two had got away in a passing vessel. Notwithstanding this statement, the truth of which I could hardly doubt, I determined to examine the island for ourselves. For this purpose the first lieutenant, with a party of 50 officers and men, landed with orders to search it thoroughly and bring off any white men that might be found. His report on returning to the ship confirmed the above account, at least so far that there was not then a white man on the island. Having the Pellew chief on board, we arrived at our former anchorage off Corror on the 16th. The next morning I despatched Mr. Carr for Arracolon, with 120 officers, marines, and musketeers, and two Englishmen as guides and interpreters, directing him to get our countrymen by peaceable means if possible, but to use his arms if he found it necessary.

The King of Corror who had on our first arrival endeavored, I believe from humane motives, to dissuade me from such an expedition, when he saw it on the point of departure, ordered his war canoes, with from four to five hundred men, armed with muskets, spears, clubs, etc., to join us and act under the orders of Mr. Carr; he himself proposing to be my companion on board, if I would permit him, until the return of the boats, thus offering his own person as a pledge that no treachery from his people was to be apprehended. After an absence of nearly four days our boats returned, bringing with them the two seamen (James Meader and Horatio King) who after much delay and difficulty were at length given up without resort to force, though obviously through the fear of it alone, for they were extremely reluctant to let them go, without the promised muskets, and seemed quite indifferent as to the fate of the chief in our hands. He was of course set at liberty, and some presents of axes, saws, etc., were made them in consideration for what they had done for Captain Bernard, and of their good treatment of the men just released.

Before closing the subject of our visit to these islands, justice requires that I should here mention the attentions we received during our stay from the worthy chief of Corror, commonly called King George, who by his uniform hospitality and kindness to strangers so well sustains the high reputation for those qualities of his ancestor, Abba Thulle. Immediately on our arrival he sent orders to the different towns and villages subject to his authority to send out their canoes and catch fish and to collect fruit and taro for us; and, besides giving us two bullocks (of which there are barely 20 on the islands), we were supplied from day to day with fish, fruit, and vegetables in the greatest abundance for all hands. Everything came in the form of presents from King George. We of course did not fail to make presents in return, which though probably of more value in their estimation than those we received, were still insufficient in ours to cancel the many obligations we felt under to this kind-hearted man.

We sailed from the Pellews on the 20th December and arrived at Lintin on the 2d January, at which time we had less than a fortnight's bread or flour, and barely three weeks' salt provisions on board the ship, from which it will be seen that our hurried movements were not without sufficient cause. Up to that period our crew had enjoyed remarkably good health. We had then only five on the surgeon's report, and those of but slight complaints. But we now very soon felt the effects of the great change of climate to which we were exposed. It was in the midst of the rainy season when we arrived in China and in the course of a few days we had as many as 62 on the sick list, of violent catarrh. In two cases, where the lungs were attacked, it proved fatal. These, with one man lost overboard, as reported in my letter from Lintin, are the only deaths that have occurred amongst us during the cruise. While at Canton I received indirectly from the acting governor of the city the usual orders invariably given to all foreign ships of war that anchor there, namely, to leave the waters of China forthwith and return to my own country. As this was understood to be a mere matter of form and without any other meaning than a simple compliance with "China custom," I took no other notice of it than to request Mr. Wetmore [probably W. S. Wetmore, an American merchant at Canton], the gentleman to whom the note was addressed to say that I intended to go to sea when I was ready. I remained a fortnight afterwards but heard no more on the subject. As it may be satisfactory to the Department to see these curious documents, I herewith enclose translated copies of them, numbered "2" and "3"; with this only remark, that there is not a word of truth in the statement of the "Pilot Tan Ying and others." No enquiries of any kind were ever made of myself or officers, nor am I aware that we were even visited by any of the authorities of the country during our stay.

We left Lintin on the 24th, stopped three days at Singapore, and, passing through the Straits of Malacca, anchored at Quallah Battoo, late in the evening of the 15th February. On the following morning I hoisted a white flag, and fired a salute of nine guns, and immediately afterwards landed, accompanied by a number of the officers of the ship. We were met on the beach by a crowd of armed men, who, though rather curious, conducted themselves in a perfectly respectful manner, and escorted us to the residence of the rajah. Our reception by this personage was polite and apparently friendly. The salute we had fired was now returned with an equal number of guns. I explained to him through an interpreter that I had called by the orders of the government of my country to pay him a friendly visit, and at the same time to see that our countrymen trading on the coast were not again molested in their lawful pursuits. He replied it was very well; he was glad to see me; said he had nothing to do with the affair of the *Friendship;* was not there at the time, nor when the place was attacked; hoped we should remain at peace. I invited him to pay me a visit on board. After hesitating some time, he asked if he could bring some of his friends with him, and being told to bring the whole town if he liked, he accepted the invitation.

Two days afterwards he came agreeably to appointment, accompanied by an escort of about 40 armed men, and bringing with him a couple of young buffaloes and some fruit as a present. I received him with a salute of 11 guns, exercised the crew at quarters, and paid him every other attention in my power. He remained on board several hours, and, when about to leave, requested me to give him a letter to be shown to others who might call there hereafter, certifying in effect that our intercourse had been of the most free and friendly character and that I was satisfied with his conduct. Such a letter was cheerfully given him. I was informed that several of our trading vessels have loaded pepper at this place since the visit of the *Potomac,* and that the trade is now carried on as if nothing had happened. Whatever injury the town may have sustained on the occasion of the attack by that ship, has since been entirely repaired, and I was assured that its defensive works are in a much better condition now, than they were at that time.

We left Quallah Battoo on the 19th, and the same night spoke an American vessel bound there. We anchored for a few days at Cape Town, and also at St. Helena. Our worthy consuls at both those places enjoined it upon me to say to the Department how desirable it was that a ship of war should occasionally pay them a visit. The frequent difficulties occurring among the crews of the different vessels (particularly whalers) that touch at their ports and which it is not always in their power to reconcile in a satisfactory manner, would, they believe, be greatly diminished and the interests of those concerned in the vessels much benefitted by the presence from time to time of a man-of-war. I received on board from the hands of those gentlemen four American seamen who were desirous of a passage home.[12]

[12] Masters' Letters, January-June, 1836, 54.

(TO BE CONTINUED.)

IX

Commerce Protection in Africa and China, *1838-1840*[1]

The cruise of the *Columbia* and *John Adams* was the ninth made to the Orient by our naval vessels in the years 1800–1840. The commander of the *Columbia* was Commodore George C. Read. As this is the last cruise to be treated in a strictly chronological order, it may be well to enumerate the ships which made previous cruises:

> *Essex,* 1800 (Chapter 2)
> *Peacock,* 1815 (Chapter 3)
> *Congress,* 1819–1821 (Chapter 4)
> *Vincennes,* 1826–1830 (Chapter 5)
> *Potomac,* 1831–1832 (Chapter 6)
> *Peacock* and *Boxer,* 1832–1834 (Chapter 7)
> *Peacock* and *Enterprise,* 1834–1837 (Chapter 7)
> *Vincennes,* 1835–1836 (Chapter 8)

The *Columbia* was the second 44-gun frigate to visit the Orient, the first being the *Potomac.* Both vessels, it so happened, were built at the Washington Navy Yard. The *Columbia* was of seven-

[1] See Letters to Officers of Ships of War, XXV, 204-206; Captains' Letters, November, 1838, 2; December, 1838, 2; January, 1839, 49; February, 1839, 14, 44; April, 1839, 40; May, 1839, 21, 101; June, 1839, 33; July, 1839, 731; August, 1839, 4; Belcher, J. H., Around the World, I, 209-336; II, 5-300; Taylor, F. W., The Flag Ship, I, 164-388; II, 9-254; Murrell, W. M., Cruise of the Frigate *Columbia;* Chinese Repository (Canton), VII, 599-656; VIII, 1-37, 57-83; and House Ex. Doc., No. 119, 26 Cong., 1 Sess.

teen hundred and twenty-six tons burden, carried four hundred and eighty officers and seamen, and cost to build four hundred thousand dollars. Her consort, the *John Adams,* was a second-class sloop of seven hundred tons burden, with a complement of one hundred and ninety officers and seamen.

Commodore Read was of Irish birth. He entered the navy in 1804, and, passing somewhat rapidly through the various grades of the line, became a captain in 1825. In the War of 1812 he served as a junior officer on board the *Constitution* and *United States,* and as the commander of the *Chippewa.* He participated in the famous fights between the *Constitution* and *Guerrière* and the *United States* and *Macedonian.* In the former, under orders from Captain Hull, he took possession of the *Guerrière* on her surrender. After his cruise to the Orient in 1838-1840 he served as commander-in-chief of the Mediterranean and the African squadrons. A few weeks before he died, in 1862, he was promoted to be rear-admiral on the reserved list.

The commander of the *John Adams,* Commander Thomas W. Wyman, entered the navy as midshipman in 1810, and died as captain in 1854. The executive officer of the *Columbia* was Lieutenant George A. Magruder, who later became a warm sympathizer with the secessionist movement, and who, in April, 1861, was dismissed from the navy, having previously served as chief of the bureau of ordnance and hydrography of the navy department. Four lieutenants of the *Columbia,* John W. Turk, Thomas Turner, James S. Palmer, and A. M. Pennock and two midshipmen of the *John Adams,* Donald M. Fairfax and Robert H. Wyman (a son of Commander Wyman), later became rear-admirals. The executive officer of the last-named ship was Lieutenant Andrew H. Foote, one of the most distinguished naval officers of the Civil War, and for a time commander-in-chief of the Mississippi squadron.

Commodore Read's sailing orders, which were dated April 13, 1838, and were signed by Secretary of the Navy Mahlon Dickerson, directed him to visit various African and Asiatic ports for the protection of our commerce. The two vessels sailed together from Hampton Roads on May 6. Separating at Rio Janeiro, they did not join each other until they reached Bombay. The *Columbia* had intended to call at the Cape of Good Hope, but owing to heavy weather near the Cape she passed on into the Indian

Ocean and did not anchor until she reached Muscat, on October 16. Here the Prince of Muscat, the third son of the Sultan, did the honors, as his father was not at the capital. He and the commodore visited each other and exchanged friendly expressions of mutual regard. He sent the commodore liberal supplies of goats, kids and fruits; and the commodore returned the favor, in part at least, by sending the Prince " some lines of poetry " in compliment of the Sultan's generous conduct toward the officers and crew of the *Peacock* and in praise of that ruler's admirable character. The poetry was the handiwork of the Reverend Fitch W. Taylor, chaplain of the squadron. From Muscat the *Columbia* sailed for Bombay.

Meantime the *John Adams* had visited Zanzibar, where Wyman and his officers found the Sultan of Muscat, who received them at his palace. " The usual congratulations were offered, " wrote one of the officers, " the Sultan expressing himself highly delighted at seeing so many of his good friends, the Americans. He inquired in polite and handsome terms after the health of the President of the United States, and was shocked to learn the political death of his old friend and correspondent, General Jackson; for he could not comprehend how an individual when once at the head of affairs could ever be anywhere else and remain in the land of the living. Of those officers of the *Peacock* whom he had seen three years before, his inquiries were anxious and friendly. He wished to know if we bore any letters from the President to himself, and, when answered in the negative, seemed quite surprised. After many interrogatories into the present state of the Ottoman Porte, the nature of the existing difficulties on the Persian frontier, and various other subjects—many of which, by-the-by, being queries belonging to that numerous class of questions more easily asked than answered—in all which his highness displayed much intelligence and political acumen, and during which he was most courteous and bland; conversation was interrupted by the entrance of some Abyssinian eunuchs bringing coffee. " This was succeeded by sherbet, both articles of poor quality. The Americans now took their leave " much pleased with the dignity of grace and benignity displayed by his highness. " [2] From Zanzibar the *John Adams* proceeded to Bombay, where she was joined by her consort.

[2] Belcher, J. H., Around the World, I, 269-270.

The British government in India extended many courtesies to the visiting squadron. Commodore Read wrote to the Secretary of the Navy:

It affords me great pleasure to be able to say that I received very polite attentions from the public authorities at Bombay. The Governor gave myself and the officers of the two ships a dinner. Lieutenant-General Sir John Keane, the commander-in-chief of the military forces, also was pleased to do the same. The Governor invited me to spend some days with him in the country, and many of the English residents called upon me. Indeed, had I stayed longer than I did, I am assured there would have been no lack of attention or want of hospitality. On the day previous to my leaving Bombay, I received His Excellency the Governor, and Sir John Keane, accompanied by their suites, on board the *Columbia* to dinner. The day passed very agreeably. The guests seemed much to enjoy themselves. Many kind and friendly speeches were made by the Governor and Lieutenant-General referring to the United States, and always concluding with the expression of the hope that the two governments might remain at peace and forever continue to be friends.[3]

Sir John Keane, who became Baron Keane of Ghuznee and of Cappoquin, was one of the principal British officers at the Battle of New Orleans, in which he was twice wounded. After his two superior officers, Generals Pakenham and Gibbs, were killed, the command devolved upon him, to whom fell the melancholy duty of leading the defeated army off the field. At the dinner at Bombay given by Read to the British functionaries, one of our naval officers in answer to an allusion by Sir John to the field of his defeat, remarked to him that " he had regained in India all that he had lost in America," to which compliment Sir John gracefully and wittily replied: " Oh, no! not quite. Tell General Jackson that I have never yet regained my former assurance of British superiority over her brothers in America, which she lost at Orleans; nor can I ever lose this Kentucky memento (striking emphatically a wound in the leg, by which he was still maimed), this parting impression which the old general made on me."[4]

From Bombay the *Columbia* and *John Adams* sailed for Goa, being the first American warships to visit that ancient seat of the Portuguese dominions in the Orient, and thence they proceeded to Colombo, Ceylon. Here another round of hospitalities were extended to the officers of the squadron. One evening they dined with the governor of Ceylon, the Right Honorable James

[3] Captains' Letters, December, 1838, 2.
[4] Belcher, J. H., Around the World, I, 336.

Alexander Stewart-Mackenzie. His wife was Maria Elizabeth Frederica Stewart-Mackenzie, formerly Lady Hood, having first married Sir Samuel Hood, vice-admiral of the white. Her second husband adopted her maiden name, Stewart-Mackenzie. In 1815 she succeeded to the family estates in Scotland and became the chieftainess of the clan Mackenzie. Sir Walter Scott refers to her as having "the spirit of a chieftainess in every drop of her blood," and "as an enthusiastic highlander in all manner of northern tradition." A glimpse of the governor and his lady as they appeared at the dinner given in honor of the Americans is presented by one of the officers of the *Columbia*:

We reached the Governor's house, a spacious mansion, at half-past seven o'clock. Commodore Read and his officers were severally presented to Mrs. Mackenzie, the Governor's lady, who entered the room with her hat on, as her head-dress, which we humbly conceive to have been in great bad taste, while her ladyship was prodigal with her smiles, and with great frankness and goodness of heart, placed her guests at their ease. The Governor's self, in lace and silver epaulets, soon presented himself, that others might be presented to him. He entered the reception room after a number of the guests had arrived, with ease, but less with the air of a polished courtier than the plainer gentleman of education and great good sense, who had seen the world and knew its different phases and its fashions.[5]

While in the midst of "all this cheerfulness and friendly intercourse," the commodore received information that an atrocious murder and robbery had been committed on board the American ship *Eclipse,* on the west coast of Sumatra, and he at once sailed for the scene of the outrage for the purpose of punishing the desperadoes. It appeared that the *Eclipse,* Captain Charles P. Wilkins, had put into Trabangan, twelve miles from Muckie, to purchase pepper; that a party of Malays had been permitted to come on board her; and that they had unexpectedly attacked the crew, killing the captain and an apprentice and wounding the second mate and several seamen. After taking possession of four cases of opium and eighteen casks of Spanish dollars, they left the ship in company with the cook, who had disclosed the hiding place of the plunder. The measures taken by Read to punish this piracy are best described in his own words:

While standing in towards Quallah Battoo, a native of Soo-soo came on board, who appeared to be well acquainted with all the circumstances relating to the case. He informed me that the plan for robbing the

[5] Taylor, F. W., The Flag Ship, I, 397.

Eclipse was devised and matured by some of the principal inhabitants of Mukkee; that it was sanctioned by the Rajahs, and carried into execution by several persons belonging to that place, who were still residing there. He informed me that several persons engaged in the perpetration of the murders and the robbery had afterwards come to Soo-soo, and were still residing there; and that one of the pirates was at Quallah-Battoo.

Having come to anchor three miles from the latter place, I deemed it my duty immediately to make the demand for the pirate and property said to have been conveyed to that place with him. Lieutenant Palmer, accordingly, was sent to the Rajah to make the demand and to say to him that the government of the United States desired to be on friendly terms with the Rajahs of Sumatra, that we had come as friends, but that it would depend upon himself whether we should, or should not, leave him with the same sentiments. The Rajah professed himself willing to comply with my wishes, but stated his apprehension that the man could not be taken for the purpose of delivering him to me; the pirate had many friends, and the people generally feared him, but he would endeavor that night to have him taken while asleep.

Commander T. W. Wyman was sent the following day, and the same excuses were repeated. The hour of sunset of the 24th was named as the limit of the time which would be allowed for the apprehension of the pirate, and the bringing of him on board the *Columbia*. The Rajah was told that unless this were done in the time specified, I should be under the necessity of considering him an enemy, and of proceeding to treat him as such; assuring him that it was impossible for him to convince me that he could not secure and give up a pirate found within the limits of his command.

The hour of sunset passed, and nothing further had been done by the Rajah in compliance with the demand. And I now conceived that all the Rajah had promised had been done for the purpose of gaining time. If I had now left him without inflicting some chastisement, I feared he might hereafter question our power, or have an indifferent opinion of its existence. I therefore caused the ships to be dropped as near to the shore as they could swing with safety; and, having sprung their broadsides to the forts, commenced a fire upon them. The fire of the ships was returned with but three shot. Two of the forts hung out white flags, and, after a few shot well directed at the Rajah's fort, I directed the firing to cease.

As I did not conceive the object for which I contended sufficient to justify the landing of a party of men to destroy the place, after they had had so much time to prepare themselves for defence, I directed the ships to be got under weigh and to proceed to Mukkee. We arrived at the common anchoring ground off that place on the evening of the 30th, and the demand for the offenders who, it was said, were residing there, was immediately made. Excuses similar to those we had before heard were now given for not having confined the persons claimed. I desired to obtain possession of the Rajahs, and invited them on board, but could not prevail on them to come. Having sent another message to the Rajahs on the succeeding day, and being satisfied that they did not mean to comply with my demands for the persons concerned in the piracy, I directed all preparations to be made for hauling in the ships.

On the morning of the first of January, we commenced towing and warping in; and by half-past 10 a. m. got into an excellent position for sweeping with our fire the peninsula on which the town stood, the two ships now not being more than a cable's length from the edge of the town. No sooner had we commenced this operation, than it was observed that the inhabitants were engaged in carrying off their property from the town. It was impossible to prevent this as early as I could have wished; but a few guns were soon brought to bear, and we saw no more persons employed in this business. A slow fire from a few guns on the main and spar deck was kept up merely for the purpose of preventing any preparations for defence, and for the protection of our men in landing. By half-past 12 p. m. three hundred and twenty seamen and marines were landed and formed on the beach, under the command of Commander T. W. Wyman. The divisions from the *Columbia* were commanded by Lieutenants Magruder, Turk, Turner and Pennock. The marines of the squadron were led by Lieutenant [D. D.] Baker. The two divisions from the *John Adams* were headed by Lieutenants [E. R.] Thompson and [George] Minor.

The firing from the ships ceased, and the expedition moved towards the town with order and regularity. Much anxiety was felt at the moment as to the result. The conduct of the Rajahs the evening before being such, it was believed that a steady and determined resistance would be made, but to my great surprise the party entered the place without opposition. The town was soon after in flames. All the dwellings of the Rajahs and their five forts were destroyed. The guns of the forts, 22 in number, found loaded and primed and matches lighted, were spiked and thrown into the ditch. A magazine of rice and a store-house filled with pepper were destroyed. Some valuable boats of large dimensions, on the stocks, and several of less value were consumed in the flames. In short there was nothing left above ground; and by half-past 2 o'clock p. m. the officers and men had returned to their respective ships, without the occurrence of a single accident.

In the performance and execution of this service, Commander T. W. Wyman exhibited a promptness and energy which could not be surpassed; and, had an enemy appeared to oppose the march of the party, his gallantry would have been conspicuous. To Lieutenant Magruder, executive officer of the *Columbia*, I feel much indebted for the good order and expedition with which the men from the *Columbia* were landed and led by him, and for the previous training they had received, the advantages of which were now apparent. Lieutenants Turk, Turner and Pennock merit my warm acknowledgments, as leaders of their separate divisions; and the conduct of Lieutenant Baker, who led the marines, deserves my unqualified approbation. Much was expected from the marines on this occasion, and much no doubt would have been done, had further proof of their skill and discipline been required. Acting Master [Edmund] Jenkins,

Midshipmen [D. R.] Crawford, [C. St. G.] Noland, [S. C.] Barney, [C. R.] Smith, [Charles] Sinkler, [W. M.] Green, [J. L.] Toomer, [C. M.] Fauntleroy, [James] McCormick, and [Edward] Donaldson, Mr. [J. Henshaw] Belcher, professor of mathematics, Mr. [John] Martin, gunner, and Mr. [Benjamin] Crow, sailmaker, were all embarked in this enterprise, and are spoken of in terms of praise by Commander Wyman, to whose report sent herewith, I must refer you for further particulars of this affair, and for the names of those officers who landed with him from the *John Adams*. He speaks in high terms of them all, and gives me every reason to believe that they merit my approbation and thanks.

The ships arrived at this anchorage [Soo-soo] on the 4th instant [January, 1839] since which time we have been busy taking in water. It was my intention on coming to this place to inflict a moderate castigation upon the inhabitants for having permitted several of the pirates to reside among them, and for not giving them up when the demand was made. But the civil and quiet manner in which they conducted themselves towards our watering party on shore, and their apparently sincere profession of inability, from want of power, to comply with my wishes, restrained me from taking such a step. Indeed, when I landed and saw the miserable places called forts by them, upon which a few four- and six-pounders were mounted, without carriages, and the guns themselves in a state of uselessness and decay, which would render it mere wantonness to attempt putting them in a worse condition, I concluded that it would be better policy to take the credit of exercising clemency towards them, and accordingly took advantage of the circumstance to make all the Rajahs of the place, with the exception of one who was absent and sick, to sign a paper which binds them to offer assistance and protection to American vessels.

Early after my return to his neighborhood, the Rajah of Quallah Battoo sent me a message by a priest of Soo-soo, to say that if I would not molest him again he would pay to the owners of the *Eclipse*, two thousand dollars (being the amount said to have been conveyed by the pirate to Quallah Battoo), at the same time declaring that he had not received a cent of the money taken from that vessel. He affirmed further that he was too poor to pay this sum at once, but that he would give his note, payable in twelve months, to any person duly authorized to receive it. As I found it impossible to obtain possession of either pirates or money, I accepted his proposition and took his note for the amount specified, the payment of which may or may not be doubtful. I gave him in return, a paper stating all the circumstances, under which the agreement was made, which he considers a treaty of peace, and I am told, values it very highly.[6]

The promissory note and treaty of peace of the Rajah of Quallah Battoo is a curious document:

This is the epistle of Po Chat Abdullah, raja of Kwala Batu, to Commander Reej, engaging to pay two thousand dollars —. As to the bad

[6] Captains' Letters, January, 1839, 49.

man, he has not been caught; he has fled. Now this agreement is to pay the said money, within twelve months, to Commander Reej, or to any other ship which shall present this writing, or another equivalent to it, whether a ship of war or a trading ship; only let not another ship make war upon the Country of Kwala Batu. Hereby is peace made with Commander Reej, and hereby does Po Chat Abdullah, raja of Kwala Batu, become his friend as long as he lives. The writing is finished. By the counsel of all the elders of Kwala Batu on the side of Achin. Our words are ended, wishing you peace and tranquility. This writing from Po Chat Abdullah of Kwala Batu is given Commodore Reej on Saturday, the 17th day of the festival month, in the year 1254. Signed as witness by Po Adam, Taku Kadang.[7]

The Rajahs of the neighboring settlements were greatly alarmed by the destruction of Muckie and hastened to make their peace with the commodore, who supplied them with " treaties. " From Sumatra the squadron went to Singapore, where a supply of provisions was obtained. As many seamen were suffering from varioloid and the bloody flux, an intended visit to Siam was abandoned, and the squadron sailed for China. During the voyage up the coast the *John Adams* parted company with her consort and called at Manila. The *Columbia* anchored at Macao on April 28, 1839. Her arrival was most opportune, for the Americans at Canton were besieged by the Chinese. Seldom indeed has one of our warships received a more hearty welcome at a foreign port. To make clear the situation at Canton, the events there of the past few months must be recounted.

For many years foreign merchants, chiefly British, though a few American, had been engaged in the highly profitable opium trade between India and China, notwithstanding the importation of that article was interdicted by the Chinese government. Many Chinese officials however, connived at the illicit traffic and shared in its profits. It was greatly increased by its being thrown open to all British merchants on the discontinuance in 1834 of the monopoly long enjoyed by the British East India Company. The opium imported into China in 1838 was valued at seventeen million dollars. It was in that year that the Emperor began to take active measures for the suppression of smuggling. He appointed Lin, one of his ablest and most energetic viceroys, high imperial commissioner, and gave him full power to stop the importation, sale and use of the proscribed drug. Lin arrived at

---

[7] Captains' Letters, April, 1839, 40, enclosure G.

Canton on March 9, 1839, and at once demanded that all the opium held by foreigners should be immediately surrendered to him to be burned, and that the foreigners should enter into "bond" assenting to the confiscation of all ships on which opium should be found, together with their cargoes, and to the punishment with death of the companies of all such ships. On March 22 the foreign trade with Canton was stopped, and shortly afterwards the foreigners were deprived of their Chinese servants. A guard was placed around the factories, all the streets (with one exception) were walled in, a double tier of armed boats was stationed in the river, and communication with Whampoa was cut off. Some five or ten thousand Chinese collected in the immediate vicinity of the factories.

The timely arrival of Commodore Read not only reassured the frightened prisoners at Canton, among whom were our consul, Mr. P. W. Snow, and several American merchants, but it also allayed the apprehension of the foreigners and native Portuguese at Macao, which place was threatened with capture or destruction. Advised by Snow, Read decided to remain at Macao, ready at any time to protect his countrymen there or at Canton, should violence be offered them. The officers of the fleet much preferred to rescue by force the prisoners at Canton, which, Read declared, "would have been more of an amusement than a trouble to us," to waiting idly in port at Macao. The feelings of the Americans is thus described by Chaplain Fitch W. Taylor:

It would be a fête gratifying, I doubt not, to all the officers of our ship, from the highest to the lowest, to force the Bogue, and to demand without delay the Americans now held within their premises at Canton. But the apprehension is, that, as their numbers are comparatively so small, and a mob of a numerous populace are ever so ready to do the bidding of the reckless and the abandoned, our approach might be attended with danger from the rabble at Canton. The authorities themselves have said, all that they have to do for the destruction of those now within their power is, to allow the mob to do their own wishes. And there may be truth in all this, as there is a general impression among the lower classes of the Chinese at Canton that the foreign factories are filled with the precious metals, and that the plunder were well worth the sacrifice of the heads of the few "foreign devils" that have the custody of it.[8]

It was fear of a massacre of the imprisoned foreigners that led Captain Charles Elliot, the British superintendent of trade, to

[8] Taylor, F. W., The Flag Ship, II, 110-111.

yield to the demands of Commissioner Lin and deliver up to him the obnoxious drug—in all, twenty-two thousand two hundred and ninety-one chests, worth about twelve million dollars. This act of Elliot postponed for a few months the conflict between Great Britain and China. On the delivery of the opium, the guard around the factories was removed, the foreigners were liberated, and trade with Canton was reopened. The British merchants, however, under Elliot's direction, left the city and did not resume their trade. The American merchants, on the other hand, remained at Canton, obtained a verbal modification of the "bond," and by July were actively engaged in commerce.

Commodore Read now felt free to depart on his homeward voyage, and resisting the importunities of Consul Snow and the American merchants to prolong his stay, he prepared his squadron to return to the United States. He was much embarrassed by the awkward situation in which he was placed by the refusal of the Chinese to recognize the authority of foreign naval officers. On one occasion when some Chinese fired most wantonly upon some Manila-men sailing under the American flag and seriously injured them, he urged Consul Snow to demand that the perpetrators of the outrage be delivered up for trial, but the consul refused to act, on the ground that it would be impolitic. Glad to be rid of his embarrassments, Read, on August 6, sailed for the Sandwich Islands. The first night out he encountered a violent typhoon which blew the sails of the *Columbia* to ribbons and drove her rapidly toward the shore to the great alarm of all on board. Happily the wind shifted in season and a disaster was averted. From Honolulu Read sailed for Valparaiso by way of the Society Islands. His voyage came to an end with the arrival in Boston of both ships in June, 1840.

X

The Opening of China,
1842-1850[9]

For more than half a century after the notable voyage of the *Empress of China,* no American vessels, unless perchance an opium smuggler or a whaler, were to be seen along the Chinese coast between Canton and Korea—some two thousand miles in extent. None of our warships had ventured to pass the Bogue and visit Whampoa and Canton. Several of them—to be exact, nine—had entered the bay of Canton and anchored at Lintin or Macao. But they were regarded as intruders, and received no official recognition from the Chinese government. The time had now arrived when the status of foreign ships of war in China was to be altered, and a serious breach was to be made in the commercial wall which that country had erected on its maritime frontier for the exclusion of foreigners and the isolation of its own citizens.

The events of the spring of 1839 culminating in the destruction of the opium at Canton by Commissioner Lin have already been described. This act of the commissioner was regarded by Great Britain as a just cause for war, and accordingly she sent a squadron to China early in 1840 to redress her wrongs. On reaching its destination, the Canton River was blockaded and one of the ports north of Canton was attacked. As these hostile operations jeopardized our commercial interests, the government at Washington decided to send a squadron to China for their pro-

[9] This chapter is based chiefly on the East India Squadron Letters, U. S. Navy Department Archives, 1841-1851; House Ex. Doc., No. 119, 26 Cong., 1 Sess.; Sen. Ex. Doc., Nos. 58, 67, 28 Cong., 2 Sess.; Sen. Ex. Doc., No. 139, 29 Cong., 1 Sess.; and the Chinese Repository, XI-XX.

tection. Two vessels were prepared for that service—the historic frigate *Constellation,* famous for her early victories under Truxtun, and the ship *Boston;* and Commodore Lawrence Kearney, a seasoned officer of the old school, was chosen to command them. During the War of 1812 Kearney was employed in protecting the coast of the Southern states, and after that war he was sent to the West Indies and to the Mediterranean to aid in suppressing piracy. In 1861 he was retired as captain, and in 1867 he was promoted to be commodore, dying about a year later, the second oldest officer of the navy.

Kearney's sailing orders were dated November 2, 1840, and were drafted by Secretary of the Navy James K. Paulding. He was directed to protect American interests and citizens on the coast of China, especially during the war between that country and Great Britain. He was to observe the laws of neutrality, and to pay due respect to the peculiar customs of the Chinese. His attention was called to the fact that the foreign and domestic policy of China differed from that of other nations, and he was instructed to avail himself of every opportunity to impress upon the Chinese people and their officials that the one great object of his cruise was " to prevent and punish the smuggling of opium into China either by Americans or by other nations under cover of the American flag." [10]

When Kearney arrived at Macao, on March 22, 1842, almost two years after the beginning of the Opium War, the British fleet was operating chiefly at Shanghai and on the Yangste-kiang, more than a thousand miles north of Canton. The British had captured Amoy, Ning-po, Tinghai and Chinhai; and had obtained possession of Hong Kong, at the mouth of Canton Bay, where they had established a naval rendezvous. They had taken the forts at the Bogue, pushed up the Canton River, and forced Canton to purchase an immunity from attack by the payment of six million dollars. Kearney arrived too late to see much of the war. The blockade at Canton had been raised, the foreign commerce resumed, and the smuggling of opium again permitted.

A few Americans had long found the trade in this proscribed article highly profitable. Indeed the foreign merchants at Canton did not generally consider this traffic disreputable, and many of them at one time or another were connected with it. When Com-

[10] Letters to Officers of Ships of War, XXX, 44-47.

modore Downes visited Lintin in the *Potomac* in 1832, one of the
officers of that frigate reported that a very fine American ship
called the *Lintin* was stationed there " to receive and dispose of
opium, of which article most of the contraband trade consists. " [11]
Our consuls, being generally merchants with commercial interests
of their own to subserve, were prone to overlook irregularities
committed by their countrymen. Kearney was the first American
official to make a vigorous attempt to suppress the traffic. A few
days after his arrival he issued the following order addressed to
the United States consular officer at Canton :

> The *Hong Kong* Gazette of the 24th instant [March, 1842] contains a
> shipping report, in which is the name of an American vessel engaged in
> carrying opium; therefore I beg you will cause to be made known with
> equal publicity, and also to the Chinese authorities by the translation of
> the same, that the government of the United States does not sanction
> the smuggling of opium on this coast, under the American flag, in viola-
> tion of the laws of China. Difficulties arising therefrom in respect to the
> seizure of any vessel by the Chinese, the claimants certainly will not,
> under my instructions, find support or any interposition on my part, after
> the publication of this notice. [12]

This edict of Kearney appeared to the British merchants, who
remembered the part played by the Americans in the smuggling
trade, especially during the opium difficulties of 1839, as a mere
affectation of high professions, and as an attempt to curry favor
with the Chinese. The fact that the British were fighting for the
interests of our commerce as well as their own, made it all the
more difficult for them to take a generous view of the edict.
Before he left China, Kearney proved to his critics that his government was acting in good faith. In May, 1843, he seized the
American schooner *Ariel,* a notorious opium smuggler, and tried
to capture the *Mazeppa* and several other illicit trafficers. Writing
to the Secretary of the Navy at this time, he said :

> The American flag is now the only cover for this illicit trade. Sir
> Henry Pottinger [the British plenipotentiary in China] having issued a
> proclamation against it; and the English craft having been turned away
> from the river, has placed the Americans in a peculiarly advantageous
> position as freighters under the flag of the United States. The British
> officers have informed me here that their subjects defy them by pointing
> to the American flag over that contraband article. [13]

[11] Reynolds, J. N., Voyage of the United States Frigate *Potomac,* 338;
Gützlaff, K. F. A., A Sketch of Chinese History, II, Appendix, Table 4;
Brinkley, F., China, X, 261-262.
[12] Sen. Doc., No. 139, 29 Cong., 1 Sess., p. 7.
[13] Sen. Doc., No. 139, 29 Cong., 1 Sess., p. 38.

Soon after his arrival at Macao in March, 1842, Kearney received several letters from American citizens demanding redress for certain outrages committed on them by the Chinese during the operations of the British near Canton in May and November, 1841. It appeared that one of our merchants, Mr. J. Coolidge, had been seized at his factory and imprisoned at Canton, and that another merchant, Mr. Morse, fearing like treatment, had made his escape to Whampoa, with rather disastrous consequences. He left the factories with two boats loaded with his property. The boat on which he embarked reached Whampoa without being molested. The second boat was attacked by Chinese soldiers, and one man, named Sherry, was killed, and the rest of the crew wounded. The survivors were captured and imprisoned in Canton. Later another boat's crew was seized and put in prison. After a brief confinement, however, all the Americans were released.

On receiving information of these outrages, Kearney decided to go to Whampoa and demand redress. On April 11, he left Macao, sailed past the Bogue, and two days later anchored at Whampoa Reach. Never before had an American ship of war, and very rarely had the national vessels of other nations, thus violated the time-honored sanctity of the inner waters of China. Strange to say Kearney's presence in the river gave no offense to the officials at Canton. On the other hand, they permitted him to disregard the roundabout method of communication hitherto strictly insisted upon, and to send his messages directly to Viceroy Ke, minor guardian of the heir apparent, president of the board of war, member of the censorate, and governor of the provinces Kwangtung and Kwangse.

On April 27 Kearney sent Lieutenant J. G. Reynolds, of the marine corps, to Canton with a letter for Ke, dealing with the outrages committed by the Chinese in 1841. Reynolds delivered this letter to the representative of the viceroy, the Kwangchauhie, the chief military officer of the department, ranking as colonel. Two days later a Chinese officer of the rank of captain delivered to Kearney on board the *Constellation* the reply of his master. The viceroy was in a remarkably conciliatory mood. He submitted the grievance of the Americans to Kearney for his decision and ordered the Hong merchants to pay the damages fixed by that officer, declaring that the firing upon and seizure of the American boats was the result of a misapprehension. While these differences were being thus amicably adjusted, a boat of the *Constellation* engaged in making soundings was fired upon by one of the Chinese forts. On learning of this additional ground for complaint, Ke explained the action of the fort satisfactorily to Kearney and degraded the officer responsible for it.

In placating the Americans, the viceroy did not hesitate to employ flattery and to overlook unpleasant truths. He referred to Kearney as an officer who " manages affairs with clear understanding, profound wisdom and great justice "; and he said that American vessels " hitherto engaged in the commerce of Canton have always been confined to the legitimate and honorable trade, and never concerned with the carrying of opium. " He gave Kearney a present of bullocks and sheep, receiving in return an atlas and several other articles of Occidental manufacture. When Kearney visited Canton and was on the point of returning to his ship, the viceroy sent one of his officers to pay a parting call and present his compliments. Never before had an American official received such polite attention from the Chinese government. This unusual conduct doubtless resulted from the determination of the government to keep on good terms with all the neutral nations of the Occident. Some weight, too, must be given to the wholesome fear of Western powers aroused by the operations of the British fleet.

While the *Constellation* and *Boston* lay at Whampoa, several high officials of the Chinese Navy visited them, and were cordially welcomed by their officers. An account of this visit was written by the Reverend E. C. Bridgman, Kearney's interpreter, and one of the first American missionaries to China.

About noon May 9, the day fixed upon for the admiral's visit, two messengers arrived to announce his approach. But it was past 2 o'clock before his barge was in sight. As he neared the ships, they were in readiness to do the honors due to his rank and station; and the manning the yards and firing of the salute, in most admirable style, were to him a sight equally novel and animating. He was received by the commodore on the quarter-deck, and conducted to the cabin. The admiral, a native of Fukien, was appointed to this station shortly after the battle of the Bogue, where his predecessor fell in the storming of one of the forts. Kwan bore a good reputation among his own countrymen; but in his appearance and whole bearing as a warrior, Wu is decidedly his superior. He is now 44 years of age, tall, well formed, has a high aquiline nose, a keen eye, and moved across the deck with an easy, but firm and manly step. He had hardly been seated in the cabin, before he begged that the men might be put at their ease—he supposing that they were then, as when he came on board, standing upon the yards. At his own request he was shown round the ship, and was afforded an opportunity of seeing the men at their quarters. The marines particularly attracted his attention; and for several minutes, while going through their evolutions, he stood like a statue fixed in perfect amazement. While the men were still at their guns, and without the admiral's knowledge, orders were given to repel boarders on the starboard quarter, where he chanced to be standing. Instantly, almost a hundred or more men, with swords and pikes and fixed bayonets, rushed up from the gun-deck, and took their proper stations. For the moment the admiral found it impossible entirely to conceal his feelings, though the lines of his face were screwed up to the highest pitch he could command. He had been forewarned of treachery by some of the wise men at the provincial city. But his fears were banished, by the men the next moment moving to the other quarter. Still more ludicrous scenes occurred at Canton. The admiral had scarcely left the city for the ship, before the senior Hong merchants were called on to give security for his safe return. And the report of thirteen guns—instead of the Chinese number three—for the salute, was such positive proof of treachery that nothing but the admiral's safe return in person could allay the alarm of the provincial authorities.

It was nearly sunset when the admiral left the ships, evidently much pleased and well satisfied with his reception, and the attentions shown him on board the foreign man-of-war. On Monday the 18th, two other officers, one the second in command to the admiral, visited the commodore. These men were from northern provinces, and though they had been a year or more at Canton, had never before been on board a foreign vessel. They said they had supposed, from all reports, that the foreign men-of-war were strong, but till then they never believed them so strong as they now found them to be. They seemed astonished when told, that many of the English ships were far superior to the *Constellation*.[14]

The age of the *Constellation* drew from the Chinese officials many exclamations of surprise, and they made "wonderful reports" of the two ships to Yih Shan, a high official at Canton. It happened that at this time Kin Ying Lin, a member of the Imperial cabinet at Peking, laid before the Emperor of China sundry drawings of warships and a recommendation for an increase of the navy. The Emperor sent the drawings to Yih Shan, who later reported, in the form of a lengthy memorial, that only vessels like those of the foreigners were at all proper for fighting, and that in the future China warships ought to be constructed after the models of the *Constellation* and *Boston*. The Emperor ordered that thereafter national ships should be of the kinds recommended. Yih Shan further reported that one vessel had al-

[14] Chinese Repository, XI, 333-334.

ready been built after a foreign model, and that two similar vessels were on the stocks.[16]

On the completion of his mission up the Canton River, Commodore Kearney about the middle of June dropped down to Macao. A month later he went to Hong Kong and exchanged civilities with the British commander there, Rear-Admiral Sir Thomas Cochrane, between whom and the commodore a good understanding existed. It was at Hong Kong that Kearney in September received news that peace had been restored, and that a treaty had been signed on August 29. The Treaty of Nanking, as this epoch-making compact was called, provided for the session of Hong Kong to the British, the payment by the Chinese of twenty-one million dollars, the opening to British merchants of Canton, Amoy, Fu-chau, Ning-po and Shanghai, the residing at these ports of British consuls, the establishment of just and regular tariffs, and the conducting of official correspondence on terms of equality.

Kearney was quick to recognize the great importance of this treaty to the United States, and, on learning its terms, he dispatched Vice-Consul Delano to Washington with a copy of it, sent duplicates overland by mail, and ordered the *Boston* to proceed to the west coast of Mexico with triplicates. He, however, did not propose to await the action of the home government. Delaying his return voyage, he set about obtaining for our merchants the same commercial privileges granted by the Treaty of Nanking to the British. " The good understanding which happily exists between the local authorities of Canton and the Americans and with myself, " he wrote to the Secretary of the Navy, " would seem to recommend this time a propitious moment for the United States to enter upon some understanding in regard to commercial privileges with the Chinese. The liberty therefore of undertaking such a measure will, I hope, find excuse even should I fail of success. "

These words were written at Macao on October 7, from which place on the following day he thus addressed Viceroy Ke:

The address of Commodore Kearney, commander-in-chief of a squadron of United States ships, respectfully represents that he learns with deep interest the high Imperial commissioners deputed to arrange commercial affairs with the British are expected in a short time to arrive at Canton,

---

[16] *The Friend of China and the Hong Kong Gazette,* December 22, 1842.

and that a commercial treaty is to be negotiated to operate in favor of "British merchants" exclusively.

The undersigned is desirous that the attention of the Imperial government might be called with respect to the commercial interests of the United States, and he hopes the importance of their trade will receive consideration, and their citizens, in that matter, be placed upon the same footing as the merchants of the nation most favored.

The undersigned does not press this matter at present, but, trusting to the good and friendly understanding which exists, he submits the case, and has the honor to be, your excellency's most obedient servant.[16]

From Macao Kearney went to Canton, where soon after his arrival he received the following favorable reply from the viceroy:

Ke, guardian of the young prince, member of the Board of War, member of the Imperial cabinet, and Governor of the two Kwang Provinces, states, in reply to the subject of the 10th of the 9th month, that I have received your polite communication relating to the English commerce. I, the governor, have ever hitherto treated the merchants of every nation with the same kindness. Moreover, the Americans who have come to Canton have had free commerce, month after month, and year after year. These merchants have been better satisfied with their trade than any other nation; and that they have been respectfully observant of the laws, is what the August Emperor has clearly recognized, and I, the governor, also well know. How, then should I not rather, on the cessation of difficulties with the English, wish to show favor to them? Now, I have ordered the Hong merchants, with the said English nation's merchants, to devise beforehand, and to wait the arrival in Canton of the Imperial commissioners, great ministers of state. When I shall have received the newly devised regulations concerning the free trade of the English, then I, the governor, together with the lieutenant-governor and Tartar General, will immediately deliberate upon the proper adjustment of the regulations, and will make a representation to the Emperor that he may hear and direct what shall be done.

Decidedly it shall not be permitted that the American merchants shall come to have merely a dry stick (that is, their interests shall be attended to). I, the governor, will not be otherwise disposed than to look up to the heart of the great Emperor in his compassionate regard towards men from afar, that Chinese and foreigners with faith and justice may be mutually united, and forever enjoy reciprocal tranquility, and that it be granted to each of the resident merchants to obtain profit, and to the people to enjoy life and peace, and universally to participate the blessings of great prosperity, striving to have the same mind.

This is my reply.

As these assurances of the viceroy were quite satisfactory, Kearney made preparations to return home, but finally decided to

---

[16] For the correspondence between Commodore Kearney and Viceroy Ke, see East India Squadron Letters, 1841-1844, 33-52; also Sen. Doc., No. 139, 29 Cong., 1 Sess., 21-36.

delay his departure, hoping that an occasion might arise for establishing a good understanding with the officials at Peking. Moreover, the English and Chinese were preparing to open negotiations respecting the new commercial system, and Kearney was of the opinion that the presence of his ship would be beneficial to America, especially should it become necessary "to make demands in favor of equal rights and commercial privileges." Pending the arrival at Canton of the British and Chinese commissioners, he visited Manila, returning to Macao on January 1, 1843. During his absence a Chinese mob attacked the foreign factories at Canton, and destroyed considerable property belonging to the American house of Augustine Heard and Company. To facilitate the settlement of the claims of this company against the Chinese government, Kearney again sailed up the Canton River; and, leaving his ship at Whampoa, went to Canton, and entered into correspondence with Ke, who gave his word that the sum claimed by the Americans should be paid. The most significant part of this correspondence, however, does not refer to these claims, but to the commercial privileges of American merchants. On this subject Governor Ke wrote as follows in a letter dated March 17:

On a former occasion, the governor received your honor, the commodore's communication, requesting him, in his behalf, to "solicit the favor of the august Emperor to allow the merchants of his honorable nation to trade upon the same terms as those granted to the merchants of other nations," etc. As in duty bound, the governor having already addressed the Emperor clearly upon the subject, waited the coming of the high commissioners at Canton, where they were in concert to attend to the foreign relations; but the Tartar General, Eleepie, having arrived at this city, but a short time elapsed, when, most unfortunately, on account of disease, he "went out of office" (i. e., deceased)—so that whatever may be just and equal in the trade of each nation, remains unsettled. It is, therefore, necessary to wait the arrival of his successor; and when some plan is adopted, then a personal interview may be held with your honor, the commodore, and, face to face, the relations between the two countries may be arranged, and the same be reported to the Emperor

In reply Kearney availed himself of the opportunity presented to say that what the Emperor "grants to the traders from other countries, his own sovereign will demand for his merchants." He assured the viceroy that he would not protect Americans seized by the Imperial cruisers in the act of smuggling opium. Respecting the proposal that the Imperial commissioner and himself should fix the commercial relations between their two countries, he said that the viceroy labored under a misapprehension, for he had not been empowered by his government to make a treaty. "If, however," he added, "his Imperial majesty will declare his will on this point, my country will no doubt rejoin to it in the same spirit of amity, and straight return an answer, and send a high officer to China, who, in connection with the Imperial commissioner, will deliberate and settle a permanent treaty of lasting peace and friendship. But to commence this good thing, to open this road of mutual benefit, belongs to his Imperial majesty of China."

Kearney's suggestion respecting the negotiation of a treaty was not approved by Ke, who said that such a compact would be contrary to Chinese custom, and would be "an unnecessary and circuitous act." He further said that the tariff of duties fixed for the English would "pass into force in a uniform manner for every country." He was not informed, however, whether the Occidental countries other than England would be permitted to trade with Fu-chau, Ning-po and Shanghai.

Before leaving China, Kearney went to Amoy, the first port north of Canton to be visited by an American warship, and thence sailed for Honolulu on his homeward voyage. He had performed the tasks committed to him with great tact, skill and firmness, and had served his country most efficiently under trying circumstances. "That little squadron," wrote the Secretary of the Navy of Kearney's command, "had done all that could have been expected of it, and it deserves much credit for its great vigilance and activity and for the prudence and sound discretion with which Commodore Kearney has acquitted himself of the important trusts reposed in him."[17] Three months after Kearney left Amoy the Imperial commissioner issued a proclamation giving to other nations the same commercial privileges granted to Great Britain by the Treaty of Nanking. The monopoly of the Hong merchants now came to an end, many antiquated restrictions on commerce ceased, and a new tariff rate amounting on the average to five per cent went into effect. For the first time China fully opened her ports and her people to intercourse with the Occident and introduced herself to the family of nations.[18]

[17] Annual Report of the Secretary of the Navy for 1842, p. 532 (in House Ex. Doc., No. 2, 27 Cong., 3 Sess.).

[18] Chinese Repository, XII, 443; Brinkley, F., China, XI, 172.

While China thus gave freely to all the Western powers the privileges Great Britain had forced from her, several of them (Belgium, Holland, United States, Spain, Portugal and France), not knowing of her liberality or unwilling to trust it, hastened to dispatch envoys to treat with her. On learning of the Treaty of Nanking in December, 1842, President Tyler sent a special message to Congress recommending the appointment of a commissioner to China, empowered to negotiate commercial arrangements. Congress did not authorize the appointment until March 3, 1843, and on the same day Edward Everett, then minister to England, was chosen commissioner. On his declining the office, President Tyler selected Caleb Cushing, an eminent lawyer, and a member of Congress from Massachusetts.

A little squadron, under the command of Commodore Foxhall A. Parker, was placed at the service of Cushing, consisting of the frigate *Brandywine,* famous for her having afforded a passage to Lafayette on his return to France in 1825, the second-class sloop *St. Louis,* Commander H. H. Cocke, and the 10-gun brig *Perry,* Commander S. F. Dupont. Commodore Parker had served in 1814 as a lieutenant on board the sloop *Adams* during her successful cruise after British merchantmen. In 1848-1849 he was sent to Germany on a confidential mission relating to the employment of American naval officers in the German Navy, then being organized. He was retired as captain in 1855, and died two years later.

The *Brandywine* and *St. Louis* were the first ships of the squadron to sail, leaving Hampton Roads on May 23, 1843. Parker gave passage to Elisha K. Kane (afterwards a navy surgeon and noted for his North Polar explorations) and four other young men, attachés of Cushing's mission, whose only duty was to add dignity and importance to it. The *Brandywine,* having parted company with her consort, arrived at Bombay on October 24, where she was joined by Fletcher Webster, the son of the Secretary of State, and the Secretary of the Mission, and by Cushing, who, after visiting London and Paris to ascertain the plans and purposes of those governments in their intercourse with China, had taken passage for India by way of Gibraltar. Webster had come out from Boston in the *Antelope,* which ship, together with another Boston vessel, the *Zephyr,* proceeded to take on cargoes of opium for the China trade. Parker was unable to discover any authority vested in him to stop their illicit trafficking.

On February 24, 1844, the *Brandywine* arrived at Macao, at which place Cushing went ashore and established the headquarters of his mission. He at once entered into correspondence with Ching, acting governor of the two Kwang provinces, residing at Canton, informing him of the powers with which he was vested. He expected to go to Peking, deliver a letter of President Tyler to the Emperor, and there negotiate the treaty. To this plan, however, the Chinese authorities firmly, though courteously, objected, and Cushing was finally induced to accept the procedure proposed by the Emperor, namely, that the treaty should be negotiated at or near Canton, and that the Chinese government should be represented by a high commissioner acting under the Imperial seal.

While Cushing was occupied with these preliminaries, Parker visited Manila, Hong Kong and Whampoa. At Hong Kong the United States had lately established a naval depot and a consulate; the former Parker moved to Macao, which port he regarded as the more convenient location. On arriving at Whampoa, he wrote to Governor Ching offering to exchange a salute of twenty-one guns, to receive the officers of the Chinese government on board the *Brandywine,* and to pay a visit of courtesy to the governor at his palace. As the war had been concluded and the fears of the Chinese somewhat allayed, Ching was much less inclined than his predecessor Ke to permit an infraction of Chinese customs. He requested Parker to withdraw immediately out of the Bogue and return to Macao. He politely declined to accept the proffered civilities, ascribing as a reason for his declination the dissimilarity between the rules of etiquette of the Central Kingdom and those of foreign nations. He attributed the breaches of Chinese custom made by the " honorable commodore " to the fact that he had never before visited the Central Flowery land, and therefore could not be expected to know its laws. Unable to satisfy the governor, Parker returned to Hong Kong.

On June 16 Kiying, the high commissioner appointed by the Emperor to negotiate with Cushing, accompanied by three distinguished officials, arrived at Casa Branca, a Chinese village adjoining Macao, and on the following day installed himself at Wanghia, just outside the walls of Macao, in a temple dedicated to the Lady of Mercy. After a few days had been spent by the commissioners in exchanging visits of courtesy, Cushing being assisted in these formalities by Parker and several of the officers of the squadron, negotiations were opened on the 21st, when the Americans submitted the draft of a treaty. Twelve days later the negotiations were concluded by the signing and sealing of the Treaty of Wanghia, by Cushing and Kiying, in the presence of Parker and the attachés of the mission. The contents of this rather lengthy document need not here be detailed. It is sufficient to note that it provided for the opening to Americans for purposes of residence and commerce of the five treaty ports, for the admission to these ports of ships of war, and for the protection of shipwrecked sailors and of vessels seeking refuge from storms.

While Parker was at Macao in the service of Cushing, he received a letter from the American consul at Canton asking for protection from a Chinese mob that had surrounded the American factory there. It appeared that the commotion had its origin in a trespass on the factory grounds committed by the Chinese. When ordered off, they refused to go. Force was used by the Americans, and in a skirmish that ensued, one of the intruders was killed. Parker at once directed a detachment of his men to proceed to Canton, but before it departed he learned that Lieutenant E. G. Tilton, the commander of the *St. Louis,* had anticipated his wishes. On arriving at Whampoa, Tilton embarked sixty seamen and marines of the *St. Louis* on board boats and conveyed them to Canton. He found a Chinese mob in possession of the grounds in front of the American factory. It, however, was easily dispersed, order was soon restored, and he shortly returned to Whampoa with his men.

On August 29, (1844) Cushing sailed for the United States on board the *Perry.* About the same time the *St. Louis* proceeded on a cruise to the North China ports and visited Chusan, still in possession of the British, and Ning-po, where she attracted much attention as the natives had never before seen an American ship of war. She returned home by way of Australia, Van Dieman's Land and New Zealand, being one of the first American warships to visit those islands. Before the *Brandywine* left Macao on December 2, for Honolulu, Parker received a communication from Kiying containing the information that the ministers of the Chinese Privy Council had sanctioned and the Emperor had approved the treaty. On the eve of his departure the Americans at Canton presented him with a superb and massive service of plate in token of their appreciation of his work in behalf of the commercial interests of the United States.

On the approval of the Treaty of Wanghia by the President and Senate, Alexander H. Everett, a distinguished American scholar and diplomat, who had been appointed to succeed Cushing as American commissioner to China, received orders to exchange ratifications with the Chinese government. A new squadron, consisting of the ship of the line *Columbus,* Captain T. W. Wyman, and sloop of war *Vincennes,* Captain Hiram Paulding, both under the command of Commodore James Biddle, a distinguished veteran of the War of 1812, was placed at the service of Everett, who, accompanied with his family, embarked on board the flagship at New York early in June, 1845. Suffering from ill health, Everett on reaching Rio Janeiro decided to abandon his mission and return home, and to transfer to Commodore Biddle his instructions from the state department and his special power to exchange ratifications with the Chinese government. The commodore arrived at Macao within a few days of the expiration of the period fixed for the execution of this formality. He, therefore, went at once to Canton, leaving his ship at Chuenpe, near the Bogue, and on December 31 the interesting event took place at Pwantang Puntong, a country seat near Canton. The Chinese were represented by Kiying, the three high officials who assisted him in negotiating the treaty, the prefect of Canton, and a large retinue of inferior officers, and the Americans by Biddle, the principal officers of the *Columbus,* Reverends Peter Parker (interpreter) and E. C. Bridgman, Consul P. S. Forbes, and several gentlemen of Canton. After the parties had passed the compliments usual on such occasions, the two ratified treaties were brought forward and were carefully compared. Being found to agree, they were exchanged in due form, Biddle presenting the document ratified by the President and Senate to Kiying, who in turn delivered to Biddle the document ratified by the Emperor; everyone standing during the ceremony. Four copies of a certificate of exchange, previously prepared in both the Chinese and English languages, were then signed and sealed by the commissioners, each of whom retained two copies. After the conclusion of the ceremonies an elaborate Chinese dinner was served in excellent style. Kiying was described by one of the Americans as an exceedingly able and accomplished man, dignified and easy in manner, comparing favorably with " the highest statesmen that can be found in any of the Western courts or cabinets. " [19]

[19] *Chinese Repository,* XIV, 590-591.

As the first treaties with China did not open Peking to foreigners, Canton became the Chinese capital for purposes of diplomatic intercourse between the empire and Occidental countries.
The Emperor sent a high commissioner to reside there, and the
representatives of the foreign governments lived there or at the
neighboring seaports. Biddle established the American legation
at the foreign settlement outside the walls of Canton, over which
he presided until April 15, 1846, when he transferred his powers
as commissioner to Dr. Peter Parker. During his stay in China
he visited Amoy, Chusan, Shanghai and Ning-po, dining at the
two latter places with the principal mandarins. He reported
that the American trade was considerable at Shanghai, but there
was little or none at Ning-po. On July 7 he sailed for Japan, and
before the end of the year both ships of his squadron returned
home.

Owing to the Mexican War none of our national vessels again
visited the Far East until the latter half of 1848, when the ship
Plymouth and sloop *Preble* arrived in China, being followed early
in 1849 by the brig *Dolphin.* This new squadron was commanded
by Commodore David Geisinger, another veteran of the War of
1812. He remained in China about a year. When in March,
1849, an outbreak of the populace of Canton was threatening
because of the approach of the date fixed for the opening of the
city to foreigners, he took measures for the defense of the factories. The opening was postponed and the commotion abated.
When in August the Portuguese governor at Macao was murdered
under circumstances of unusual atrocity, he landed a small force
at that place to protect the Americans and their property. The
usual cruises to the Northern ports of China were made, and our
commerce at Shanghai was reported to be prosperous and rapidly
increasing.

In February, 1850, Geisinger, having been succeeded by Com-
modore P. F. Voorhees, returned home in the sloop of war *St.
Mary's,* which had brought out the new commander-in-chief.
After a brief and uneventful tour of duty, Voorhees sailed from
China for the United States in August, leaving only one ship on
the station, the sloop of war *Marion,* Commander W. M. Glendy.
Voorhees's successor, Commodore J. H. Aulick, did not arrive in
China until February, 1852.

On the opening of the five treaty ports, our trade with China
and the number of Americans residing in that country gradually

increased. About 1840 the number of our merchantmen annually
visiting Canton was sixty. In 1849 one hundred and three vessels
entered the ports of Canton, Shanghai and Amoy. One-fourth
of our trade was with Shanghai. The number of arrivals of
American ships in China was one-third that of the British, and
with the exception of Great Britain greatly exceeded that of any
other foreign nation. Immediately after the Opium War there
began to appear in Chinese waters long, trim vessels, whose nar-
rowness of beam, sharp lines, tall masts, large spars and heavy
weight of canvas appalled the old salts of the trade. These were
the China clipper ships, that greatly reduced the time of voyage
between the Occident and the Orient, vying with each other to
be the first to deliver the early teas in London and New York.
So superior were the first American clippers to their British rivals
that they almost monopolized the carrying trade between China
and London. [20]

Soon after the Treaty of Wanghia went into effect, American
consulates were established at Amoy, Fu-chau, and Shanghai.
The first American consul at Hong Kong was appointed in 1843.
The first American missionaries in China were the Reverends E.
C. Bridgman and David Abeel who arrived at Canton in 1830.
When the ports to the northward of Canton were opened to foreigners on the termination of the Opium War, American missions
were established there, and the number of missionaries in the
treaty ports rapidly increased. The total number of Americans
in China, however, was not great. In 1850 it amounted to about
two hundred, some thirteen per cent of the Occidental population.

[20] Speer, William, The Oldest and Newest Empire, China and the United States, 417-419.

(TO BE CONTINUED.)

XI

First Voyages to Japan, *1846, 1849*[1]

A half century after the Europeans began to navigate the Indian Ocean about the year 1500, the Portuguese and Spanish opened up a considerable trade with Japan. They were soon followed by the Dutch and English, who by the first part of the seventeenth century had almost monopolized the commerce between Japan and the Occident. In the meantime Roman Catholic missionaries had entered the land of the Mikado and were pursuing their calling with their usual zeal and bigotry. Finally, after welcoming the aggressive Westerners for upwards of a century, Japan entered upon a policy of non-intercourse with them, largely as a result of the strife engendered by the missionaries. In 1621 she forbade her citizens to visit foreign countries, and three years later she banished from her domain all Westerners, with the exception of the English and the Dutch. Twenty years later she limited her Western trade to the Dutch, and permitted them to visit only the island of Deshima, near Nagasaki. Here the Dutch erected a factory and established a small settlement, which was presided over by a general agent or superintendent. The natives were forbidden to visit the island, and the foreigners were not allowed to cross the small bridge which connected it with

---

[1] See East India Squadron Letters, 1845-1847, 37, 60-62; 1848-1850, 124-129, 194-263; Sen. Doc., No. 59, 32 Cong., 1 sess.; Nitobe, I. O. The Intercourse between the United States and Japan, 7-37; Chinese Repository, VI, 209-229, 353-380; XV, 172-180; XVIII, 315-332; Logs of the *Columbus, Vincennes* and *Preble,* U. S. Navy Department Archives; Proceedings of the United States Naval Institute (Annapolis), XXXI, 555-563; The Independent (New York), LIX, 407-501, 1043-1044; and Nordhoff, Charles, Nine Years a Sailor, 194-208.

Nagasaki. At first the Dutch were granted permission to send eight ships annually to their factory, but in time this number was reduced to two, and finally to one.[2]

During the Napoleonic wars, the Dutch, in order to avoid exposing their own vessels to capture by British cruisers, employed neutral ships to make the annual voyages to Deshima. It was owing to this practice that some of our merchantmen were afforded an opportunity to visit Japan—the first American ships to enter the waters of the Mikado. During the years 1797-1809, the Dutch hired no less than eight American vessels to make voyages from Batavia to Deshima: the *Eliza,* of Boston, Captain W. R. Stewart; *Franklin,* of Boston, Captain J. Devereux; *Massachusetts,* of Boston, Captain W. V. Hutchings; *Margaret,* of Salem, Captain Samuel Derby; *Samuel Smith,* Captain G. Stiles; *Rebecca,* Captain J. Deal; *America,* Captain Henry Lelar; and *Mount Vernon,* Captain J. Davidson. In Japanese waters these ships sailed under the Dutch flag, as otherwise they would not have been permitted to conduct the Dutch trade. The first account of Japan from the pen of an American was written by Mr. George Cleveland, the captain's clerk of the *Margaret.* The first two voyages were made by the *Eliza* in 1797 and 1798.

The captain of the *Eliza,* W. R. Stewart, appears to have been a shrewd Yankee, with a sharp eye for the main chance, for after completing his contract with the Dutch, he in 1803 sailed boldly into Nagasaki, under the American flag, with a cargo purchased in Bengal and Canton. He asked the Japanese permission to trade and to obtain some water and oil. The first request was positively refused, but the second was granted; and, after his wants had been supplied, he was ordered to depart. Four years later another American vessel, the *Eclipse,* visited Nagasaki, under circumstances that aroused the suspicion that she came to trade, rather than to obtain refreshments, professedly her object. She too was denied the rights of commerce, and on being furnished with provisions was permitted to continue her voyage. During the thirty years immediately succeeding the visit of the *Eclipse,* our merchantmen seem to have respected the desire of the Japanese to be left alone.[3]

[2] Nitobe, I. O., The Intercourse between the United States and Japan, 7-25; Adams, F. O., The History of Japan, I, 69.

[3] Doeff, H., Herinneringen uit Japan, 61-62, 153-157; Chinese Repository, X, 162.

The first American whale ship to enter Japanese waters made its appearance off the coast of Japan in 1820. In the following year some six or seven of these venturesome craft cruised there, and in 1822 more than thirty. It is highly probably that the early whalers sought refreshments on shore or anchored in some sheltered port to escape heavy weather.[4]

In 1837 the American firm of Olyphant and Company, of Canton, made an attempt to induce the Japanese to relax their exclusive commercial policy. It decided to transport to Japan some ship-wrecked subjects of the Mikado who had been brought to Macao, and to avail itself of the opportunity thus afforded for producing a favorable impression upon the Japanese government. The expedition was placed in charge of Mr. Charles W. King, an American merchant, and the American ship *Morrison,* Captain David Ingersoll, was chosen to make the voyage. For purposes of trade, a small assortment of cloth, adapted to the Japanese taste, was put on board, and several presents illustrative of the American civilization were added. As the object of the voyage was a peaceful one, the guns of the *Morrison* were removed. The expedition first proceeded to Yedo Bay, where it was fired on by the batteries on shore, and was not permitted to communicate with the government at Yedo. Thus foiled, it sailed southward to the bay of Kagoshima, and there it met with a similar reception. Forced to abandon its mission, it returned to China with the shipwrecked sailors, who on witnessing the hostile temper of their countrymen did not care to land.[5]

In 1846 a voyage similar to that of the *Morrison* was made by Captain Mercator Cooper, of the whaler *Manhattan,* of Sag Harbor, Long Island. While on a cruise to the whaling regions of the North Pacific, Cooper landed at St. Peter's Island, a few degrees southeast of Japan, and found there eleven shipwrecked Japanese sailors. He offered to convey them to their native land, and they gladly consented to go. On his way thither he rescued eleven more Japanese from a floating wreck. Arriving on the coast of Japan, he sent messengers to inform the Emperor of the object of his visit and of his desire to enter the harbor of Yedo. The Emperor gave his permission to visit the capital, and

---

[4] Davis, J. F. China during the War and since the Peace, II, 281; King, C. W., and Lay, G. T., The Claims of Japan and Malaysia upon Christendom, I, 75.

[5] Chinese Repository, VI, 209-229, 353-380.

on his arrival there treated him with much civility, supplying him with wood, water and provisions, and making him a present of some Japanese crockery, some lacquered ware and a specimen of the Emperor's writing. Cooper and his crew were forbidden to leave their ship and were commanded never to come again to Japan. He held several conversations with the governor of Yedo and other officials of rank, and after a stay of four days, having landed the shipwrecked sailors, left the bay.[6]

The first voyages of our merchantmen to Japan preceded by several years the first voyage of our national vessels. The earliest connection between the navy and Japan, if we may accept the authority of De Bow's Review, may be seen from the following item extracted from this journal for December, 1852: " This [expedition to Japan] has been long in contemplation by our government. Com. Porter, as far back as 1815, addressed a letter to Mr. Monroe [Secretary of State] on the subject, and it was then intended to send out Com. Porter with a frigate and two sloops of war, but the plan was defeated." Unfortunately this quotation, so far as it refers to Porter, stands unverified, and there is much doubt whether that officer ever proposed such an expedition.[7]

The first official action of the United States respecting Japan was taken in 1832 when Mr. Edmund Roberts, who had been ordered by the State Department to negotiate treaties with the rulers of Cochin China, Siam and Muscat, was authorized to institute a separate mission to Japan, provided he found the " prospect favorable." Should the mission be instituted, he was to take passage in a coasting vessel, under convoy of the sloop *Peacock*, since, to make the voyage in a ship of war would subject him to the indignity of having his vessel disarmed, in accordance with Japanese custom. For some reason, he decided not to make the proposed visit.

In 1835, when about to leave Washington on his second embassy to the Orient, Roberts was directed to go to Japan and attempt to open negotiations for a treaty with the Emperor of that country. The entering of some other port than Nagasaki, the Japanese permitting, was recommended, as the Dutch had an establishment there and they might feel themselves interested in thwarting him. In case he obtained a treaty, permission was

[6] Chinese Repository, XV, 172-179.
[7] De Bow's Review (New Orleans), XIII (1852), 560.

granted him to give the Japanese presents to the value of ten thousand dollars. He was furnished with a letter from President Jackson addressed to the Emperor and with numerous gifts, including a gold watch with a heavy gold chain eight feet long, a sabre, rifle and shot-gun, a pair of pistols, an assortment of broadcloth, some cut glass, a music box, some maps, a set of American coins, prints of American naval victories, and ten Merino sheep of the finest wool. On the death of Roberts in 1836, soon after reaching Macao, the Japanese mission was abandoned.[8]

The American missionaries and merchants in China early recognized that Japan offered a promising field for their activities, and were greatly interested in the measures proposed for the opening of that country to the outside world. They, in all probability, brought to bear their views on Commissioner Caleb Cushing during his six months' stay in China. However that may be, it was inevitable that so sagacious a diplomat as Cushing should, on making a treaty with China, conceive the idea that Japan might be induced to follow the example of her neighboring empire. He communicated his views on this subject to President Polk, who, although believing that the probability of effecting a commercial arrangement with Japan was small, authorized John C. Calhoun, the Secretary of State, to transmit to Cushing full powers to treat with the Japanese government. Cushing left China before he received Calhoun's letter, and the duty of undertaking the mission developed upon Alexander H. Everett, his successor as commissioner to China. Owing to sickness, Everett transferred his powers to Commodore James Biddle, who, however, was otherwise authorized to visit Japan, as may be seen from the following extract taken from his sailing orders dated May 22, 1845:

You will hold the squadron at the disposal of the Commissioner, for the purpose of conveying him to any part of the coast of China or Japan, which he may have occasion to visit in the execution of his instructions. . . . . In an especial manner you will take the utmost care to ascertain if the ports of Japan are accessible. Should the Commissioner incline to make the effort of gaining access there, you will hold your squadron at his disposition for that purpose; and should he decline to do so, you may yourself, if you see fit, persevere in the design, yet not in such a manner as to excite a hostile feeling or distrust of the Government of the United States.[9]

[8] Foster, J. W., American Diplomacy in the Orient, 140-141; Sen. Doc., No. 59, 32 Cong., 1 sess., p. 63.
[9] Confidential Letters, U. S. Navy Department Archives, I, 126.

Biddle was one of the oldest and most distinguished officers of the navy, his name being seventh on the navy list of 1845. He was a nephew of Captain Nicholas Biddle, who lost his life during the Revolutionary War by the blowing up of his ship, the frigate *Randolph,* during an engagement with the British vessel *Yarmouth.* Young James entered the navy in 1800. In the war with Tripoli he served as a midshipman on board the *Philadelphia* and was imprisoned at Tripoli on the capture of that vessel. In the War of 1812 he was a lieutenant on the *Wasp* when she captured the *Frolic,* and the commander of the *Hornet* when that vessel took the *Penguin,* receiving for the latter victory a gold medal from Congress. After the War of 1812 he took possession of the country bordering on the Columbia River in behalf of the United States, and he served as one of the representatives of his government in negotiating its first treaty with Turkey.

Biddle's little squadron consisted of the ship of the line *Columbus,* the only vessel of that class to visit the Far East, and the sloop of war *Vincennes,* Captain Hiram Paulding, now making her fourth cruise to the Orient. On this voyage the *Columbus* sailed sixty-nine thousand miles, establishing a record for a ship of her class. On her return home she was laid up in ordinary at the Norfolk navy yard, where she remained until the outbreak of the Civil War, when she was scuttled and sunk to prevent her from falling into the hands of the Confederates.

Biddle's duties in China, which have been described in the previous chapter, occupied him several months, and the summer of 1846 had arrived before he was ready to visit Japan. On July 7 he sailed with both vessels from the Chusan Islands, near Shanghai, for Yedo, which port he had decided to enter in preference to Nagasaki, where such opposition as the Dutch might offer would have to be encountered. On the 19th, on approaching Yedo Bay, he passed several Japanese junks, which gave him a wide berth, and on the following day he entered the bay, carefully picking his course by means of soundings and a lookout. When some twenty-five miles from Yedo, a Japanese officer, accompanied with a Dutch interpreter, boarded the flagship and motioned to the commodore that he had gone far enough. Not wishing to give offense, Biddle anchored at the place pointed out, which was on the south side of the bay, abreast a village. The adjacent country was beautifully green, and appeared to be well cultivated.

As soon as Biddle had anchored, he was surrounded by numerous boats, and many Japanese came on board the ships, a freedom that he permitted in order to convince them of his friendship and of his ability to defend himself.

Soon after the officer boarded the *Columbus,* he held a conference with the commander-in-chief. " He inquired what was was my object in coming to Japan," Biddle wrote to the Secretary of the Navy, " I answered that I came as a friend to ascertain whether Japan had, like China, opened their ports to foreign trade; and if she had, to fix by treaty the conditions on which American vessels should trade with Japan. He requested me to commit this answer to writing, and I gave him a written paper, a copy of which is herewith transmitted. He informed me that any supplies I might require would be furnished by the government. To my inquiry whether I would be allowed to go on shore, he replied in the negative." [10]

On the morning of the 21st another officer, apparently of higher rank, came on board the flagship. " He stated," said Biddle, " that foreign ships upon entering a port of Japan always landed their guns, muskets, swords, etc. I told him it was impossible for us to do so, that trading vessels only could be expected to do so, and I assured him that we were peaceably disposed, so long as they were. He informed me that my written paper of the preceding day had been transmitted to the Emperor, who was some distance from Yedo, and that an answer would be received in five or six days. I asked him why we were surrounded by boats, and he replied that they might be ready in case we wanted them to tow the ship. This, of course, was not true; the object, of course, being to prevent our communicating with the shore. When our boats were sent to sound at some distance from the ship, Japanese boats followed them, without, however, molesting them. During our whole stay these boats continued about the ship. I had on board copies, in Chinese, of the French, English and American treaties with China. I offered these treaties to the Japanese officer, who declined receiving them, saying that he could not receive them without the permission of his Emperor. I offered these treaties subsequently to other Japanese officers, who in like manner declined to receive them."

[10] For Biddle's account of his visit to Japan, see Sen. Doc., No. 59, 32 Cong., 1 sess., pp. 64-66.

The Japanese furnished the fleet with wood, water and provisions, refusing in accordance with their customs to accept remuneration. In watering the ships they at first sent off only small quantities. Annoyed by their procrastination, Biddle said to one of the officers that if they did not water the ship properly he would obtain a supply by sending his boats ashore. This threat had the desired effect, bringing forth an abundance of water. Concerning the eatables supplied by the Japanese, Mr. Charles Nordhoff, first-class boy on the *Columbus,* wrote thus:

> An intimation having been given that some fresh provisions would be highly desirable, two large junks made their appearance from the upper harbor, bringing to us a supply of vegetables of various kinds and several hundred chickens. Among the vegetables were sweet potatoes, egg plants, carrots, and pumpkins. There was also a quantity of small green apples, the first we had seen since leaving home.[11]

On the 25th Biddle, not having received an answer to the paper sent on shore five days previous, expressed his surprise to one of the Japanese officers at the delay, and requested him to inform the governor of Yedo that he wished an answer as early as possible. On the 27th an officer, accompanied with a suite of eight persons, approached the flagship in a junk, bringing the reply of the Emperor, and asked the commander-in-chief to come aboard the junk to receive it. An unfortunate occurrence now took place, which rather reflects upon the discretion of Biddle, as may be seen from his own account:

> I refused, and informed the interpreter that the officer must deliver on board this ship any letter that had been entrusted to him for me. To this the officer assented, but added, that my letter having been delivered on board the American ship, he thought the emperor's letter should be delivered on board the Japanese vessel. As the Japanese officer, though attaching importance to his own proposal, had withdrawn it as soon as I objected to it, I concluded that it might be well for me to gratify him, and I informed the interpreter that I would go on board the junk, and there receive the letter. The interpreter then went on board the junk. In an hour afterwards I went alongside the junk in the ship's boat, in my uniform; at the moment that I was stepping on board, a Japanese on the deck of the junk gave me a blow or push, which threw me back into the boat. I immediately called to the interpreter to have the man seized, and then returned to the ship. I was followed on board by the interpreter and a number of Japanese officers. They all expressed the greatest concern at what had occurred, stated that the offender was a common soldier on

[11] Nordhoff, Charles, Nine Years a Sailor, 205.

board, and assured me that he should be punished severely. They asked in what manner I wished him punished, and I replied, " according to the laws of Japan." I stated that the officers were greatly to blame as they ought to have been on deck to receive me. They declared that they had not expected me alongside, and I was subsequently convinced that, owing to bad interpretation, they believed my final decision had been that they were to come to the ship. I was careful to impress upon all the enormity of the outrage that had been committed, and how much they owed to my forbearance. They manifested great anxiety and apprehension, and endeavored in every way to appease me. In the course of the day, the governor of Yedo sent an officer to inform me that the man should be severely punished, and that he hoped that I would not think too seriously of the affair. The conduct of the man is inexplicable, especially as all the Japanese in and about the ship had evinced great good nature in all their intercourse with us."

The delivery of the Emperor's letter was finally made on board the *Columbus* by the Japanese officer, who was accompanied by the Dutch interpreter and his suite. The letter was without address, date, signature, or seal. These omissions indicated not so much disrespect for the Americans as an unwillingness to have official intercourse with them and a desire to discourage their return. The letter was partly written in Chinese, and partly in Japanese, in accordance with the reputed usage of Japan. It was enclosed in a cover upon which were the words " explanatory edict," a term applicable only to an act of the Emperor. As translated by the American legation at Canton, it read as follows:

The object of this communication is to explain the reasons why we refuse to trade with foreigners who come to this country across the ocean for that purpose.

This has been the habit of our nation from time immemorial. In all cases of a similar kind that have occurred we have positively refused to trade. Foreigners have come to us from various quarters, but have always been received in the same way. In taking this course with regard to you, we only pursue our accustomed policy. We can make no distinction between different foreign nations—we treat them all alike; and you, as Americans, must receive the same answer with the rest. It will be of no use to renew the attempt, as all applications of the kind, however numerous they may be, will be steadily rejected.

We are aware that our customs are in this respect different from those of some other countries, but every nation has a right to manage its affairs in its own way.

The trade carried on with the Dutch at Nangasacki is not to be regarded as furnishing a precedent for trade with other foreign nations. The place is one of few inhabitants and very little business, and the whole affair is of no importance.

In conclusion we have to say that the Emperor positively refuses the permission you desire. He earnestly advises you to depart immediately, and to consult your own safety by not appearing again upon our coast.[12]

When the substance of this admirably plain, clear and dignified statement of Japanese custom and polity had been translated to Biddle by the Dutch interpreter, he said to the officer that the United States wished to make a treaty with Japan, but not unless Japan also wished a treaty; that he came to Yedo for information on this subject; and that, having ascertained that the Japanese were not yet prepared to open their ports to foreign trade, he should sail on the following day. The officer asked Biddle to commit his answer to writing, a request that was readily granted.

On the morning of July 29, after an interesting stay of ten days in Yedo Bay, during which time hundreds of Japanese visited the *Columbus* and *Vincennes,* Biddle ordered the anchors to be weighed. To hasten his departure, several hundred native boats, the wind blowing light, towed the ships out to sea. He left the Japanese rejoicing at having rid themselves so easily of their unwelcome guests. The *Vincennes* returned to China, and the *Columbus* went to the west coast of America, which she reached in time to participate in the Mexican War.

Mr. Alexander H. Everett, the American commissioner to China, was of the opinion that Biddle's attempt to open negotiations with the Japanese " placed the subject in a rather less favorable position than that in which it stood before." Another eminent authority, Commodore Stephen B. Luce, a midshipman on the *Columbus,* takes the view that Biddle's courteous and conciliatory bearing toward the Japanese predisposed them to look with favor upon those Americans who subsequently visited their country. The statements of both Everett and Luce may be in a measure correct. In consenting to go aboard the junk, Biddle was evidently indiscrete, and the incident was used by the natives to discredit the Americans. On the other hand, the presence of an armed fleet in the bay of Yedo and Biddle's amicable and judicious relations with the Japanese officials gave them a favorable impression of the strength, candor and justice of the great Western republic. Biddle must be awarded the distinction that attaches to the pioneer, for he was the first American naval officer to anchor a fleet in the waters of Japan, to hold intercourse with the officials

[12] Sen. Doc., No. 59, 32 Cong., I sess., p. 68.

of that country, and to acquire a firsthand knowledge of its people and customs. Those who came after him had the advantage of his experience.[18]

After Everett's return home from Rio Janeiro in 1845, his health improved, and in the following year he went to China and entered upon his duties as commissioner. He was again granted power to negotiate a treaty with Japan, but died before an opportunity for exercising it presented itself. During the term of office of his successor, Mr. John W. Davis, an occasion arose for sending a national vessel to that country. Davis, on being notified by the consul of the Netherlands at Canton, on the authority of the Dutch superintendent at Deshima, that fifteen American sailors were imprisoned at Nagasaki, advised Commodore David Geisinger, the commander-in-chief of the East India squadron, to send a vessel to Japan to obtain the release of the prisoners. Accordingly, on January 31, 1849, Geisinger ordered the national ship *Preble,* Commander James Glynn, to proceed at once to Nagasaki and demand the surrender of the fifteen sailors and of any other Americans confined in Japan. In case he failed at Nagasaki, Glynn was to go to Yedo and communicate with the Imperial court respecting the sailors. He was directed to be " conciliatory, but firm," and to pay due respect to the Japanese laws and customs.

Glynn's voyage to Japan was the chief event of his naval career, which otherwise was not especially notable. He entered the navy from Virginia in 1815, and reached the grade of lieutenant in 1825, commander in 1841, and captain in 1855. In 1861 he was retired as captain, and four years before his death, in 1871, he was promoted to be commodore on the retired list. In February, 1848, he took command of the *Preble* at Callao, and in May sailed from San Blas for Macao, with Commodore Geisinger on board. The *Preble* was rated as a 16-gun sloop, and on her voyage to Japan carried one hundred and forty-one men.

The sailors, whose release Glynn was ordered to obtain, had belonged to the American whaler *Lagoda,* Captain John Brown, of New Bedford. In June, 1848, they deserted their vessel on the northwest coast of Japan, and after cruising along the shore several days, were arrested by some Japanese officers and taken to

[18] Sen. Doc., No. 59, 32 Cong., 1 sess., 15, 19, 69; Proceedings of the United States Naval Institute XXXI, 557.

Matsumai, where they were imprisoned. Thence in accordance
with Japanese law, they were conducted to Nagasaki and confined there. They were suspected by the Japanese of being spies,
and their repeated and often successful attempts to break jail
confirmed the suspicion. During their imprisonment, which was
somewhat rigorous, one of them hanged himself, and another
died of fever. Mr. J. H. Levyssohn, the superintendent of the
Dutch factory at Deshima, interested himself in the unfortunate
men, relieving their most urgent wants and communicating a
statement of their case to the Dutch consul at Canton. Five of
the men were Americans and ten Sandwich Islanders.

The *Preble* sailed from Hong Kong on February 12, 1849, but
was obliged soon to return to port owing to the appearance of
small pox on board, and did not again go to sea until March 22.
After calling at the Lu-chu Islands where she spent three days,
she finally, on April 17, made land near Nagasaki. On the following day, having anchored some distance from the town, she
was boarded by a Japanese officer, Moreama, accompanied with
eigth "assistants." Moreama spoke English, and at once conferred with Glynn, who assumed a tone and manner that he maintained uniformly throughout his stay. Believing that Biddle's
dealings with the Japanese had been too kindly and conciliatory,
he decided to try the efficacy of rigorous firmness, cool assurance,
and a severity of demeanor. When Moreama asked, " With all
respect, may I be informed of your object in coming to Japan,"
Glynn evaded the question, saying that he came on important
business with the government. To Moreama's next question,
" Did you receive a paper?" Glynn replied: " No; one of your
boats came alongside, and threw on the deck of this ship a bamboo
stick, in which was stuck a paper. If this paper was intended for
me, it was not the proper manner to communicate with me, and I
ordered it to be immediately thrown overboard. I am ready to
receive all communications which come to me in a proper and
respectful manner." Moreama said that his purpose in boarding
the ship was to acquaint its commander with the proper anchorage, which he pointed out on a chart. Glynn now raised objections, saying that his present anchorage and the one pointed out
were unsafe, that in order to secure his ship in case of heavy
weather it was necessary for him to anchor her inside the harbor,
and that he intended, on the departure of his visitors, to get

under way and stand in. After parleying over the point for a time, Moreama yielded it, and the *Preble* was anchored in the harbor, abreast the island of Happenberg, below the town and the Dutch factory, with which places communication was by boat.[14]

At Nagasaki the arrival of Glynn caused great commotion. Some six thousand troops were assembled there, the forts of the town were strengthened with recruits, and a cordon of boats was placed around the *Preble* to prevent communication with the natives. Forbidden to visit the strange vessel in the harbor, the Japanese used the battlements of Nagasaki as a vantage-point from which to view her. Not the least excited of those on shore were the American prisoners, whose spirits revived at the prospect of release.

Soon after the ship reached her anchorage near the island of Happenberg, she was boarded by a " high military chief," Serai Tatsnosen, who was accompanied by Moreama as interpreter. After ascertaining that the visitor's rank and credentials were satisfactory, Glynn entered into conversation with him, answering his questions respecting the purpose of the mission and the character of the ship. The visitor also had some interesting information to impart, namely, that an American of whom Glynn had had no previous knowledge was confined at Nagasaki, and that two of the *Lagoda's* sailors were dead. He offered to furnish gratuitously any refreshments of which the *Preble* stood in need, but Glynn refused to accept them unless permitted to pay for them, which permission was refused.

On the 19th a second high military chief, Matsmora Schal, visited the American commander to present the compliments of the governor of Nagasaki and that official's congratulations on the safe arrival of the *Preble*. After answering the visitor's questions respecting the objects of the voyage of the *Preble,* her dimensions, the age of her commander, and the size of the American navy, Glynn presented him with a letter for the governor requesting the release of the prisoners. On the 22d Matsmora Schal returned to say that the governor had received the letter. Glynn asked him when an answer was to be expected and whether the men were to be given up, but was unable to obtain a satisfactory reply. On the same day, the 22d, a message was received

---

[14] For the principal documents relating to the voyage of the *Preble,* see Sen. Doc., No. 59, 32 Cong., 1 sess., pp. 2-63.

from Levyssohn stating that the governor had requested him to translate Glynn's letter; that he had intimated to the governor the necessity of releasing the men; and that, impressed with the fact that the governor could not legally act on their case without a special order from the Emperor at Yedo, he had proposed that the men be delivered to him at the factory to be conveyed thence to the *Preble*.

On the 23d Serai Tatsnosen returned to the ship, and an interview took place in which Glynn spoke with unusual candor and brusqueness. His speech had also a note of Occidental conceit and superiority, such as has often marked the intercourse of the Western peoples with those of the East. It was evidently intended to operate upon the fears of the Japanese. Glynn thus describes the dialogue between himself and his visitor:

Chief to Commander Glynn.—I am happy to see you, sir. The ship-wrecked Americans, as I stated to you in my conference of the 18th, are in Nangasacki. I have come to-day to say that Mr. Levyssohn called upon the governor of Nangasacki in relation to the demand contained in your letter to the governor for the release of your countrymen. Mr. Levyssohn begged the governor to set aside the usages of Japan, which must (if the governor insisted upon them) keep the Americans here until a period of thirty-five or forty days should elapse, and to give the men to the officer who had been sent for them; that he (Mr. L.) would take the men and deliver them to the commander of the *Preble,* etc., etc. I have come to tell you that day after to-morrow Mr. L. will call and see you on board your ship.

Answer.—Sir, I am obliged to you for your politeness, and hope you are well. I have heard what you have said. I am displeased at it. I cannot stay here from day to day under such pretences. I have other duties to perform, and it is necessary my business should be despatched quickly. You say that Mr. Levyssohn has "begged the governor," etc., etc. I, too, beg that my shipwrecked countrymen should be restored to their homes. But understand me, I came here to treat with your governor, not with Mr. Levyssohn, or any other individual. I am under positive orders to demand from the governor of Nangasacki the release of the Americans in his hands. I want to know decisively if I am to get the men. I want the chief to reply to my question.

Chief.—This cannot be. Why not stay a few days? You will get the men, I think.

Question by Commander Glynn.—Do you say that I can get the men day after to-morrow?

Answer.—No; not day after to-morrow. The day after to-morrow Mr. Levyssohn will come and see you on this business, and afterwards, I cannot say how long, I think you will get your sailors. Mr. Levyssohn will send you a letter to-day.

Question.—Well, your answer is very far from satisfying me. It is necessary for me to see Mr. Levyssohn. Then I will go now, and call on him at Decima.

Answer.—You cannot, for he is sick.

Question (to the interpreter).—Is it necessary for the governor to get permission from the Emperor before giving up the men?

Answer.—Yes.

Commander Glynn to the interpreter —" Yes." Well, that is enough for me to hear.

Interpreter.—But stop; pray hear me. What do you do so for (alluding to the gestures of Commander Glynn)? It is not good, it is not Japanese custom.

Commander Glynn.—Well, it is my custom. It is the custom of my country, under such circumstances; and if it is necessary to send to the Emperor before giving me these shipwrecked men, I cannot stay here. My government knows very well how to recover its citizens. You need not point to your chief. I am as great as he is. You must look me in the face when speaking to me. So far as I am concerned, this matter is settled. You need say no more. I do not know any one in this business except the governor. I know no other person; nor do my orders require that I should speak to any one but the governor. If you will promise that on the day after to-morrow the men will be given up, then I will stay. If this promise cannot be given, then I have no farther business here; my errand is at an end. I will get under way to-day—yes, in five minutes—and report to my government that you decline complying with my demand for the release of the men.

Answer (with much trepidation).—Mr. Levyssohn will call on you in two days. I will do all I can, and exert my influence with the governor to give you the men soon. "I think" you may expect it and—

Commander Glynn.—Stop! Your policy is very apparent. Now, I do not want to know what you "think"; you have had ample time, certainly, to think. I can think also. I have thought a great deal. It is time that matters should come to a crisis—that something definite was arrived at. I have been here five days—a time full enough for the governor to have come to some determination, and to have sent me a reply to my letter. You put me off from day to day on the merest pretences, and up to this moment you refuse to let me know if my demands are to be denied, or not. I want a "positive promise" as to whether I am to get the men or not. Under such a promise I will give two days; more I must not, cannot give. Will you give me this promise?

Answer.—I cannot promise. I think after you have seen Mr. Levyssohn, you will get the men soon.

Commander Glynn.—I understand very well the meaning of this delay, nearly as well as you do. I think I will go to the governor myself, and there can be no better time than to-day. Can I see him?

Answer.—No; you cannot go to the governor. I will tell the governor and do all I can to have your business finished. In two days you cannot get the men—in three days, I think. Day after to-morrow Mr. Levyssohn will speak to you. He has talked with the governor about it.

Commander Glynn. It is useless to talk to me in this manner. I want no prevarication. I want a straight up and down answer. I have already waited five days—four days too long; and now I want to know something more than " I think." You give a direct reply to my question, and I will do the thinking. I will stay three days—certainly no longer—but you must promise me now that in three days you will deliver up the men. Do you promise?

Answer.—Yes; in three days you shall get possession of the men—I mean the day after the second day from now.

Commander Glynn.—Very good (offering his hand to the chief, who took it). I rely upon your word—upon the solemn promise of a Japanese chief. I place full confidence in your honor. I believe that you will fulfil your promise.

During the whole of this conference, there was a constant reference by the interpreter to the principal chief, " Tatsnosen," and his associates. The conference ended, the chief walked around the ship, inspected the crew at general quarters, etc.[15]

From the speeches of the Japanese official, it is evident that the governor had accepted the suggestion of Levyssohn. On the 25th the Dutch superintendent, being still sick, sent his representative to the ship to present Glynn with an official account of the confinement of the prisoners. This was much more favorable to the Japanese than the account given by the prisoners, who claimed to have been harshly treated. On the following day a high military chief, Hagewara Matasak, appeared on board the *Preble,* chiefly for the purpose of making this brief speech to Glynn: " To-day you will get your countrymen. After they come on board your ship, it is the verbal order of the governor for you to go away." Levyssohn's representative and another Dutchman from Deshima next arrived, and they presented Glynn with some papers from the Japanese government. Shortly after they left, a boat flying the Dutch flag came alongside the *Preble* and delivered fourteen sailors—thirteen of them from the *Lagoda,* and one, Ranald McDonald, from the American whaler *Plymouth,* of Sag Harbor. Desirous of obtaining a knowledge of the Japanese, McDonald had, at his own request, been set adrift in a boat on the coast of Japan, and, after an experience similar to that of the deserters of the *Lagoda,* was taken to Nagasaki.

On the morning of the 27th the *Preble* sailed for Shanghai, where she arrived six days later. Notwithstanding the signal success of Glynn's mission, he seems to have received no marks of official favor or appreciation. Some credit for its success doubt-

[15] Sen. Doc., No. 59, 32 Cong., 1 sess., pp. 35-36.

less belongs to Levyssohn, who well merited the thanks tendered him by Glynn. The visit of the *Preble* to Japan marked a distinct advance in our intercourse with that country. While the *Manhattan* had returned some Japanese to their native land, the *Preble* had performed the much more difficult task of obtaining the release of Americans confined in Japan.

XII

The Opening of Japan,
1851-1854[16]

The philosophical historian, powerless to predict with accuracy before the event, but wonderfully wise with explanations after it, is likely to discover numerous " causes " of the opening of Japan. He finds the times ripe for loosening the fetters that bound that country to an obsolete policy, and the circumstances unmistakably pointing toward America as the country destined to achieve the great work. Thus, a young Japanese author, schooled in the historical method of an Occidental university, enumerates the following as causes leading to the inception of the American expedition : on the one hand, the safety of American whalers on the coast of Japan, the rise of industrial and commercial commonwealths on the Pacific, the discovery of gold in California, the increasing trade with China, the development of steam navigation necessitating coaling depots and ports for shelter, the opening of highways across the Isthmus of Central America, the missionary enterprises on the Asiatic continent, and the rise of the Hawaiian Islands ; and on the other hand, the knowledge of foreign nations among the ruling classes of Japan, the news of the British victory in China, the progress of European settlements in the Pacific, the dissemination of Western science among a progressive class of Japanese scholars, and the advice of the Dutch government to discontinue the antiquated policy of exclusion.[17] These

---

[16] This chapter is based chiefly on the East India Squadron Letters, 1851-1855; Sen. Ex. Doc., No. 59, 32 Cong., 1 sess., pp. 57-62, 73-82; No. 34, 33 Cong., 2 sess.; American Historical Record, III, 148-149, 294-296; Hawks, F. L., Narrative of the Expedition of an American Squadron to the China Seas and Japan, Vol. I ; Spalding, J. W., Japan and Around the World, 101-344; Taylor, Bayard, A Visit to India, China, and Japan, 360-465; Nitobe, I. O., The Intercourse between the United States and Japan, 38-54; and Griffis, W. E., Matthew Calbraith Perry, 281-374.

[17] Nitobe, I. O., The Intercourse between the United States and Japan, 38-39.

are undoubtedly pertinent facts, and from them it may be seen that the opening of Japan by the United States, like every other historical happening, bears a definite relation to certain antecedent conditions; but they by no means prove that the event flowed irresistibly out of those conditions. Had Great Britain, and not the United States opened Japan, the philosophical historian would have discovered in that fact no reason for astonishment, but on the other hand he would possibly have explained it as the inevitable effect of numerous causes, such as the gradual extension of British influence in the Far East, the predominance of Great Britain in Oriental commerce, her opening of China in 1842, her several attempts to open Japan, her surveys of Japanese waters, and the need of her shipwrecked seamen cast away in Japan for protection.

To a writer who is somewhat skeptical of the probative value of historical causes, it will not be necessary to go far afield in explaining the decision of the American government in 1851 to make another attempt to establish commercial relations with Japan. On January 6 of that year Mr. Aaron H. Palmer, of Washington, wrote a letter to President Fillmore, in which he recommended the sending of a mission to Japan, entrusted to a special commissioner and supported by an imposing squadron. Fillmore referred this letter to his Secretary of State, Daniel Webster, with whom Palmer several times conferred respecting his proposal. In January, 1851, the *Preble* arrived at New York, and Commander Glynn shortly went to Washington, where he doubtless laid before the government the details of his cruise and urged upon it the need of the United States for a coaling depot in Japan, a project he strongly favored. In June, under order from the President, Glynn prepared a statement of his views respecting the opening of Japan.

Early in May Commodore J. H. Aulick, who had been selected to succeed Commodore P. F. Voorhees, as commander-in-chief of the East India squadron, and who was then preparing his flagship, the *Susquehanna*, for a voyage to China, proposed to Secretary Webster that the returning to their native land of several Japanese sailors who had been picked up at sea and had been brought to San Francisco might afford a favorable opportunity for establishing commercial relations with Japan. Webster was favorably impressed with Aulick's proposal, and he at once

brought it to the attention of President Fillmore, who, after dis-
cussing it with his cabinet, decided to establish a mission to Japan,
to entrust it to Aulick as an envoy of the United States, and to
empower him to negotiate a treaty with the Japanese government.
In a letter from Fillmore to the Emperor, dated May 10, 1851,
the objects of the proposed negotiations were stated to be the
establishment of friendly commercial intercourse and the obtaining of a coaling depot. A letter of credence from Fillmore to
Aulick was dated May 30, and Aulick's instructions from Webster
bore the date of June 10. These latter he probably did not receive
until he reached his station, since he sailed from Old Port Comfort
on June 8.[18]

As Aulick had suggested the mission, and as he had previously
visited the Far East, his appointment to negotiate a treaty with
Japan was a most fitting one. His squadron was composed of
three vessels, the flagship *Susquehanna*, Captain William Inman,
and the sloops of war *Plymouth*, Commander John Kelly, and
Saratoga, Commander W. S. Walker. The *Susquehanna* was a
steam frigate, bark-rigged, and was the first American steam
vessel of war to visit the Orient. Secretary of the Navy Graham
regarded this small fleet as quite sufficient for the performance of
the duties entrusted to Aulick. To the secretary, the expedition
to Japan was merely incidental to the regular work of the squadron, and no special preparations for it were made. On the outward voyage Aulick conveyed several distinguished passengers
to Rio Janeiro, namely, the Chevalier S. de Macedo, minister of
Brazil to the United States; Mr. Robert C. Schenck, United
States minister to Brazil, and Mr. J. S. Pendleton, charge d'af-
faires to the Argentine Republic.

Unfortunately for the commodore, and mainly as a result of his
irascibility, some unpleasant incidents occurred on the voyage to
Rio Janeiro and after reaching that city. He and his captain
quarreled over their respective duties on shipboard, and so serious
were their differences that each wrote to the Secretary of the Navy
making charges against the other. Aulick asked the secretary
either to detach Inman or to allow him a commander, adding that

[18] Palmer, A. H., Documents and Facts Illustrating the Origin of the
Mission to Japan, 5, 22; Davis, G. L., Origin of the Japan Expedition, 7;
American Historical Record, III, 148-149, 294-297; Sen. Ex. Doc. No. 59,
32 Cong., 1 sess., 57, 74, 80-82; Executive Letters, U. S. Navy Department
Archives, January-May, 1851, 123.

if neither of these requests could be granted, he wished to be relieved from his command at the earliest day consistent with the good of the service. Greatly incensed at the quarrelling officers, the secretary sharply reproved both of them, using these words in a letter to Inman:

Were it not that the public interests might suffer by the recall of the *Susquehanna,* the Department would not hesitate to order her return for the purpose of relieving the two senior officers as wholly disqualified, under the temper which they have evinced, to carry out any important instructions of their government."

During the voyage to Rio Janeiro, Minister Schenck discovered, or thought he discovered, certain facts gravely reflecting upon the conduct of Aulick, and he therefore wrote to the State Department making a "painful and mortifying" disclosure respecting that officer. He charged him with allowing Minister Macedo to make the passage to Rio Janeiro under the impression that he was being entertained at the expense of the commander-in-chief, when as a matter of fact the United States government was paying for his entertainment. The whole affair was trivial, and should never have been made the subject of a communication to the State Department. Schenck's charges reached Secretary Webster about the middle of November, 1851, and he at once forwarded them to Secretary Graham, who on the 17th of that month wrote to Aulick asking for an explanation. On the following day, as the President had in the meantime decided to remove Aulick from his command "in order to satisfy Brazil," Graham wrote again, directing him to remain at Hong Kong or Macao until his successor as commander of the squadron should arrive there.

These letters reached Aulick a few days after his arrival in China, and, astonished and mortified beyond measure, he at once replied to Schenck's charges, denying them absolutely and supporting his denials by the testimony of his officers. Ill at ease, and often incapacitated for duty by sickness, he remained on his station more than a year, awaiting the arrival of his successor. Finally, in March, 1853, he left China for America, taking the overland route and stopping at London. On reaching Washington he requested the Secretary of the Navy to institute an official investigation of his conduct, if he were dissatisfied with the explanations already made to the Department. The secretary assured him that the explanations were " full, complete and satisfactory," and that the ordering of a naval court was not deemed necessary. It later appeared, however, that Schenck's charges were partly true, for Macedo had been under the impression that Aulick was paying for his mess aboard ship, a misapprehension that arose from no intentional deception on the part of his host.

Aulick's tour of duty in the Far East was his last sea service. In 1867 he was promoted to be commodore on the retired list, and three years later he died in Washington. To the end of his life his recall was a sore point, and he never forgave the Navy Department for snatching from him the honor of opening Japan, which he conceived to be practically within his grasp.[19]

On the same day that Secretary Graham wrote to Aulick to await in China the arrival of his successor, he addressed a letter to Commodore Matthew C. Perry, who was stationed at New York, ordering him to proceed at once to Washington to confer with the Department. When Perry arrived at the capital, Graham and Secretary Webster were too busy to discuss with him his selection as Aulick's successor, the purpose of his visit. Graham therefore directed him to return to his station and await the instructions of the Department. Shortly after his return, he wrote a letter to Graham expressing his views respecting the proposed assignment of duty. He said that he much preferred to be commander-in-chief of the Mediterranean squadron, since in time of peace that office was the most desirable in the gift of the Secretary of the Navy, and the one conferring the most honor. He was willing, however, to accept the office offered to him provided the sphere of action of the East India squadron and its force were so enlarged "as to hold out a well-grounded hope of its conferring distinction upon its commander." He was of the opinion that the object of the government respecting Japan could not be attained without greatly augmenting the fleet in the Eastern seas.

On January 14, 1852, Graham again ordered Perry to report at the Department in Washington. It was probably before that date that President Fillmore considered the subject of the Japan mission with his cabinet; and (quoting his own words used in 1874) "it was finally determined to send an expedition expressly to Japan and Commodore Perry was selected to take the command. Instead of sending a single ship, it was thought best to send a

[19] Executive Letters, June-December, 1851, 74; Confidential Letters, II, 267-268; East India Squadron Letters, 1851-1853, 155-170; National Intelligencer (Washington), Dec. 19, 1853; Jan. 3, Jan. 9, 1854.

somewhat formidable and imposing fleet, as the show of power might be deemed a persuader with that people in procuring a treaty." [20]

Commodore Perry belonged to a family already distinguished for its naval achievements before he shed lustre upon it. His father, Captain C. R. Perry, had served in both the Revolutionary navy and the early navy under the Constitution, and his brother, Commodore O. H. Perry, had won the victory at the battle of Lake Erie, which he announced in those well-known words: " We have met the enemy and they are ours." In the War of 1812 Matthew C. Perry had served as a subordinate officer on board the frigate *President,* and after that conflict he had had a varied career at sea and on shore, assisting in the suppression of piracy, in founding a colony in Africa, in establishing a steam navy and a naval apprentice system, and in improving the naval ordnance. In 1843, as commander of the African squadron, he pursued, with remarkable success, a " powder and ball " policy in dealing with the natives of the west coast of that continent, and during the Mexican War he commanded one of the largest squadrons ever assembled under the American flag. At the time of the expedition to Japan he was fifty-nine years old, having spent forty-three years in the navy.

On March 24, 1852, Secretary Graham formally directed Perry to take command of the East India squadron, then consisting of the *Susquehanna, Plymouth* and *Saratoga,* in China. To these ships were added the steam frigate *Mississippi,* the first-class steamer *Princeton,* and the storeship *Supply.* The *Mississippi,* Perry's flagship in the Mexican War, was designated as the flagship of the squadron until the commodore should reach his station. She was one of the pioneer steam vessels of the navy, having been built in 1841. She was burnt and sunk on the river that bears her name in 1863.

During most of the year 1852 Perry was busy preparing for his expedition. The procuring of charts and books relating to Japan early engaged his attention, and in the spring he visited Albany, Boston and New Bedford in the interest of his mission. The governor and officials of New York gave him several valuable publications of that State, and the textile manufacturers of Massa-

[20] American Historical Record, III, 149; Letters to Officers of Ships of War, XLVI, 226, 332; Captains' Letters, July-December, 1851, 136.

chusetts supplied him with specimens of cloth. From numerous sources he obtained curios, arms and various articles illustrative of the progress of the mechanical arts. At New Bedford the owners and masters of whaling ships gave him information respecting the cruising grounds and the usual ports of resort of their vessels. Two artists and an agriculturist were engaged, and rated as officers of the navy, as Perry was resolved to admit no one on board his ships who was not subject to naval discipline. He was exceedingly careful to select able and discrete officers. Commander H. A. Adams was made captain of the fleet, and Commanders Franklin Buchanan and Sidney Smith Lee received important offices. Lieutenants John Contee and Silas Bent were attached to the *Mississippi* as flag lieutenants, the last-named having served with Glynn on the *Preble*.

The *Supply* was the first ship to sail, leaving New York in May (1852). The *Princeton* and *Mississippi* were not ready until fall, by which time the Department had decided to add to the squadron the ship of the line *Vermont*, the corvette *Macedonia*, the steamer *Alleghany*, the sloop of war *Vandalia*, and the storeship *Southampton*. On November 8 President Fillmore and Secretary of the Navy Kennedy visited the *Mississippi*, then at Annapolis, to bid the commodore good bye. A few days later she proceeded to Norfolk where she was joined by the *Princeton*. The latter vessel on her passage from Baltimore down the Chesapeake proved to be so defective that Perry decided to go to sea without her, and accordingly on November 24 he sailed from Norfolk for China, with a single ship of his squadron, the *Mississippi*.

Before his departure, Perry received from the government at Washington the various official documents relating to his mission: a letter of credence signed by President Fillmore; a letter addressed to the Emperor of Japan signed by Fillmore, countersigned by Secretary of State Edward Everett, and drafted by Secretary of State Daniel Webster, who had recently died; sailing orders from the Navy Department; and instructions from the State Department, bearing the signature of Acting Secretary of State C. M. Conrad. The last-named document expressed best the expectations of the government. The objects of the expedition were stated to be, first, the protection of American seamen and property in Japan and Japanese waters; second, the opening of one of or more ports to American vessels for the obtaining of supplies, and third, the opening of one or more ports for purposes of trade. Perry was directed to try first the efficacy of argument and persuasion. If he failed by the use of these means, he was to change his tone and inform the Japanese in the most unequivocal terms that the American government would insist that all its citizens who temporarily sought refuge in Japan on account of shipwreck or stress of weather should be treated with humanity, and that it would chastise severely any one who should practise upon them acts of cruelty. He was to bear in mind, however, that the President had no power to declare war, that the mission to Japan was necessarily of a pacific character, and that force was not to be used except in self-defense. The coasts of Japan and the adjacent islands were to be surveyed, provided it could be done without interfering with the main object of the mission.[21]

The American government made no secret of the expedition to Japan, which, before Perry left the United States, had assumed the importance of an international event, arousing the interest of the whole civilized world. The public prints both at home and abroad commented freely upon it, generally wishing it good fortune, but gravely expressing their forebodings of failure. The *London Times* doubted " whether the Emperor of Japan would receive Commodore Perry with most indignation or most contempt." Rumors were circulated that the expedition was not a wholly pacific one. Joking on this aspect of it, *Punch* declared that Perry must open the Japanese ports even if he had to open his own. A Washington correspondent of the Baltimore *Sun,* comparing the sailing of Perry's fleet to the sailing of " Rufus Porter's aerial ship," insisted on the " abandoning of this humbug, for it has become a matter of ridicule abroad and at home." [22]

Before leaving the United States, Perry had pretty thoroughly familiarized himself with the literature relating to Japan, and during his voyage he continued his studies and also matured a plan of operations. From Madeira he wrote to the Secretary of the Navy recommending as a preliminary step in the negotiations the securing of one or more ports of resort in Japan or in the Lu-chu Islands. The President authorized him to carry out his recommendation, at the same time cautioning him to " make no

[21] Sen. Ex. Doc., No. 34, 33 Cong., 2 sess., pp. 7-8.
[22] Nitobe, I. O., The Intercourse between the United States and Japan, 43-44.

use of force, except in the last resort for defence." The President also approved another suggestion of Perry, the encouraging of the natives in the neighborhood of the ports of resort to turn their attention to agriculture in order that they might provide themselves with the means of supplying vessels.

On the outward voyage the *Mississippi* touched at Madeira, the Cape of Good Hope, Mauritius and Singapore for supplies, and finally arrived at Hong Kong on April 7, 1853, about a month after Aulick relinquished his command. Perry found on the station the *Susquehanna, Plymouth, Saratoga* and *Supply.* After visiting Canton and engaging the American missionary, Dr. S W. Williams, as interpreter, he proceeded to Shanghai, where he assembled all his vessels, except the *Saratoga,* which he left at Macao under orders to await the arrival of Dr. Williams and join the fleet at the Lu-chu Islands. In the latter part of May all the vessels of the squadron, with the exception of the *Saratoga* which was left at Shanghai to guard American interests, arrived at Napa, Great Lu-chu Island. As the commodore had decided to make Napa a port of refuge, he spent several days there cultivating the friendship of the natives. On June 6, accompanied by a suite of officers, he visited the prince-regent at his palace and was hospitably received. During the stay of the fleet at Napa an exploring party, in charge of the Reverend George Jones, the chaplain of the *Mississippi,* penetrated the island in search of scientific information, and the harbors of Napa and Melville were surveyed.

While awaiting the arrival of a collier from Shanghai, Perry with the *Susquehanna* (now the flagship) and *Mississippi* visited Port Lloyd, Peel Island, situated some eight hundred miles eastward of Nagasaki. Here he purchased a tract of land for a coaling depot, surveyed the harbor, explored the island, and distributed some live stock and garden seeds among the settlers. After a brief stay he returned to Napa.

Finally the preparations were completed; and on the morning of July 2 the squadron, consisting of the steamers *Susquehanna* and *Mississippi* and the sloops of war *Saratoga* and *Plymouth,* set sail for the bay of Yedo, one thousand miles east-northeast of Napa. Perry had fully considered the policy that was to govern his dealings with the Japanese, and had fixed definitely its general lines. He decided not to resort to force, unless it was absolutely necessary. Those courtesies which were due from one civilized nation to another he should demand as a right and not solicit as a favor. He should permit no petty annoyances, disregard all threats, and confer only with functionaries of the highest rank. By keeping himself in the background, surrounding his person with an air of mystery, and insisting upon elaborate formalities, he should strive to impress the Japanese with the importance of his mission and to win their respect.

On the morning of July 8, as the ships approached Yedo Bay, their decks were cleared for action, the guns were placed in position and shotted, and the crews were called to quarters. About five o'clock in the afternoon the fleet anchored off the town of Uraga on the west side of the bay, twenty-seven miles from the capital. It was immediately surrounded by Japanese boats, one of the most conspicuous of which came alongside the flagship, and a Japanese officer asked for the commander-in-chief. On learning that the rank of the officer was only that of a vice-governor, Perry refused to see him, but appointed Lieutenant Contee to confer with him. For this interview and the events of the following day, Perry's narrative is the best authority:

He was merely told, under instructions from me, that I had been sent on a friendly mission to Japan, with a letter from the President of the United States for the Emperor, and it was my desire to have a personal interview with a dignitary of the highest rank, in order to make arrangements for the delivery of copies and translations of the documents with which I had been charged, preparatory to the formal presentation of the originals.

He replied that Nagasaki was the only place, according to the laws of Japan, for negotiating foreign business, and it would be necessary for the squadron to go there; to which he was told that I had come purposely to Uraga, it being near to Yedo, and should not go to Nagasaki; that I expected the letter to be duly and properly received where I then was; that my intentions were perfectly friendly, but I would allow of no indignity, nor would I permit the guard-boats, which were collecting about the ships, to remain where they were, and if they were not immediately removed, I would disperse them by force. On having this interpreted to him, he suddenly left his seat, went to the gangway and gave an order which caused most of the boats to return to the shore; but a few of them remaining in clusters, an armed boat from the ship was sent to motion them away, at the same time showing their arms, which had the desired effect, all of them disappearing; and we saw nothing more of them near the ships during the remainder of our stay. Here was the first important point gained.

The vice governor shortly after took his leave, saying that he had no authority to promise anything respecting the reception of the President's letter, but in the morning an officer of higher rank would come from the city, who might probably furnish some further information.

On the following morning, the 9th, the governor of Uraga, Kayama Yezaimon, came on board, thus giving the lie to the vice governor, who declared himself of the highest authority in the city; and as this officer was of superior rank to the visitor of the day before, I directed that he should be received by Commanders Buchanan and Adams and Lieutenant Contee, still refusing to receive myself any one but a counsellor of the empire (cabinet minister).

The governor, after a long discussion in which he more than once declared that the Japanese laws made it impossible that the letter should be received at Uraga, that the squadron must go to Nagasaki, and even if the letter of the President were to be received at this place, a reply would be sent to Nagasaki. In answer to this he was told I would never consent to such arrangement, and would persist in delivering it where I then was; that if the Japanese government did not appoint a suitable person to receive the documents addressed to the emperor, I would go on shore with a sufficient force and deliver them, whatever the consequence might be.

On this being communicated to him, he said he would return to the city and send a communication to Yedo asking for further instructions; that it would require four days to obtain a reply; upon which he was told that I would wait until Tuesday, the 12th, three days, when I should certainly expect a definite answer. Accordingly he left the ship with the understanding that there would be no necessity for any further discussion until the time appointed for the delivery of the answer from Yedo should arrive.

At this interview the original letter of the President, together with my letter of credence, were shown to the governor, encased as they were in the magnificent boxes which had been prepared at Washington, the exquisite workmanship and costliness of which evidently surprised his excellency, and, on leaving the ship, he made an offer for the first time of supplies of water and refreshments, but was told that we did not stand in need of anything.

I had directed that a surveying boat, well manned and armed, from each ship of the squadron, should commence at daylight this morning, the 9th, the survey of the harbor and bay of Uraga, and thinking it quite possible, they might meet with some resistance, I instructed Lieutenant Silas Bent, in command of the surveying party, not to go beyond the range of our guns, and caused a lookout to be kept upon them, that assistance might be sent should they be attacked; but though they were followed by numbers of Japanese boats, they did not, on seeing our men well armed, venture to molest them.

The governor inquired what these boats were doing, and, on being told they were surveying the harbor, he said it was against the Japanese laws to allow of such examinations; and he was told that, though the Japanese laws forbade such surveys, the American laws command them, and that we were as much bound to obey the American as he was the Japanese laws. Here was a second and a most important point gained.[23]

The following day, July 10, being Sunday, no communication was had with the officials. Early in the morning of the 11th, Perry ordered the surveying boats, under convoy of the *Mississippi,* to proceed farther up the bay toward Yedo, hoping thus to alarm the Japanese and induce them to give a satisfactory answer to his demands. Presently the governor came on board the *Susquehanna,* and asked why the vessels were sent up the bay. He was informed that, as the anchorage at Uraga was unsafe and inconvenient, a more favorable one was being sought nearer to Yedo, which the squadron would use the coming season, should it be necessary to return to Japan at that time.

On the morning of July 12, the day on which an answer from the Emperor was expected, the governor came on board the flagship, accompanied with two interpreters. He said that a misunderstanding had arisen respecting the proposed plan of the Americans to deliver first the translations and later the originals of the official documents. After much discussion, Perry consented to deliver both at the same time, provided a dignitary of the highest rank was appointed to receive them. The governor agreed to this, and said that an appropriate building for use as a council-house would be· erected. He further stated that the Emperor's answer would be sent to Nagasaki to be delivered to the Americans by either the Dutch or Chinese superintendent there. Perry replied that he would not go to Nagasaki, that he would receive no communication through the Dutch or Chinese, and that he expected a reply of some sort to be delivered to him in Yedo Bay.

The place selected for a meeting was the village of Kurihama, near Uraga. At first Perry opposed this selection, saying to the Japanese that one of the houses or forts opposite the anchorage of his ships would be acceptable to him. Later, however, when informed by his surveying party that the fleet could be brought within gunshot of Kurihama and that large numbers of the natives were to be seen completing the building and transporting to it furniture and other articles, he made no further objections. On the 13th the governor presented the credentials of his highness, Toda, prince of Idzu, the representative of the Emperor,

[23] Sen. Ex. Doc., No. 34, 33 Cong., 2 sess., pp 46–47.

and they proved to be satisfactory. On the following morning
the whole fleet was anchored in line so as to cover with its guns
Kurihama and the adjacent shore. Under date of July 14 Perry
has this entry in his notes:

This being the day appointed for my reception on shore, and every
preparation having been made for landing a formidable escort composed
of officers, seamen, and marines, from the respective ships, about 400 in
number, all well armed and equipped; and being ready for disembarca-
tion, the two steamers moved to a position commanding the proposed
landing-place (the sloops of war not being able to move for want of
wind), and shortly after the detachment forming, the escort were in the
boats and on their way to the shore, where they landed and formed, and
were immediately followed by me.

The whole shore of the bay, extending more than a mile, was crowded
with Japanese troops—from five to seven thousand—drawn up under arms.
These troops were composed of cavalry, artillery, infantry and archers;
some of the infantry with flint muskets, others with matchlocks.

On landing, I proceeded at once to the building erected for the purpose,
and was there received by the prince of Idzu, first counsellor of the emperor, and his coadjutor, the prince of Iwami. To the former of these I
presented the President's letter, my letter of credence, and three communications from myself, together with transcripts of the same in the
English, Dutch, and Chinese languages, for which the prince of Idzu gave
me a receipt.

The princes were attended by the governor of Uraga, the chief interpreter, and a secretary.

As it was understood that there was to be no discussion at this meeting,
I remained but a short time, taking my departure and embarking with the
same ceremony with which I had landed.[24]

To the commodore's concise account a few facts illustrative of
the brilliant pageantry of the meeting may be added. At the
head of the American party was a company of marines commanded by Major Zeilen; following them was a stalwart boatswain's mate, bearing the broad pennant, which was supported by
two tall athletic seamen; then came two boys especially dressed
for the occasion carrying in a envelope of scarlet the box containing the official documents; and next came the commodore with
two black body guards, his staff, a suite of officers, two standard
bearers, a company of sailors gaily uniformed, and the band of the
Mississippi. The official documents were of folio size, beautifully
written on vellum, and bound in blue silk velvet. Each seal was
attached by cords of interwoven gold and silk with pendant gold
tassels, and was encased in a box of rosewood, with lock, hinges

[24] Sen. Ex. Doc., No. 34, 33 Cong., 2 sess., pp. 50-51.

and mountings of gold. As a receptacle for the documents the Japanese had prepared a large lacquered box of a scarlet color, and supported by feet of brass or gilt.

The meeting place was a room in a thatched building, entirely open on one side and draped with gauze curtains. One the left of the room as you entered it were seated the princes of Idzu and Iwami, and behind them a considerable number of two-sworded mandarins. The prince of Idzu was garbed in a maroon silk robe, an over-garment of red, and blue cloth socks. His suite were attired in much the same manner. On the right side of the room were some ornamental chairs, placed there for the use of the Americans.

The conference opened with a few minutes of complete silence, both parties being seated. Tatznoske, the pricipal interpreter for the Japanese, was the first to speak, asking Mr. A. L. C. Portman, the Dutch interpreter of the Americans, if the documents were ready for delivery, and informing him that the prince of Idzu was ready to receive them. On this being interpreted to the commodore, he beckoned to the two boys, who came forward bearing the handsome boxes, and followed by two stalwart negroes. On reaching the receptacle prepared by the Japanese, the boys handed the boxes to the negroes, who opened them, took out the documents, and after displaying the writing and the seals laid them upon the lid of the receptacle. Under instructions from the commodore, Mr. Portman indicated to Tatznoske, who with the governor of Uraga was kneeling, the character of the several documents. Tatznoske then arose, and approaching the prince of Iwami prostrated himself and received from the prince a roll of papers, then crossing the room he fell on his knees before the commodore and presented him with it. After an interval of silence the commodore directed his interpreter to inform the Japanese that he would leave within a few days with the squadron for the Lu-chu Islands and Canton, to offer them his services if they wished to send dispatches, and to say that it was his intention to return again in the spring. When the Americans arose to depart, the two princes also arose and remained erect while their visitors filed out of the building, still preserving an absolute silence.

The roll of papers presented to the commodore by Tatznoske was an Imperial receipt for the President's letter, which, the receipt stated, was received at Uraga, in opposition to Japanese law, because a refusal would have insulted the ambassador of the President. The receipt closed with these words. " The letter being received, you will leave here." To show the Japanese how little he regarded their command, Perry, on returning to the flagship, proceeded toward Yedo with the whole fleet, a part of it resuming the work of surveying the bay. On July 15 and 16 the surveys were continued, and the boats of the *Mississippi* made soundings within six miles of the capital. The nearer the Americans approached Yedo, the more polite and friendly the Japanese became. On the 16th the governor brought numerous presents to the flagship, which Perry consented to accept on the condition that he be permitted to return the courtesy. The governor raised the invariable objection that the Japanese law forbade the acceptance of favors from foreigners, but he finally yielded, returning to the shore with gifts exceeding in value that of those he brought. " Here," wrote Perry, " was another point gained in the unprecedented circumstances of their consenting to exchange presents."

Perry's decision not to wait for a reply to the President's letter, but to return to China and come again in the spring was not only stated verbally to the princes, but was also committed to writing and sent to the Emperor. In reaching this decision he was moved by several considerations. It seemed best to him to give the Japanese government ample time for reflection and discussion, and not to press it for an immediate answer when it could offer valid excuses for refusing one. Moreover, his fleet was in need of coal and refreshments, the situation in China called for the presence there of several vessels, and by the following spring re-inforcements from America would have arrived on the station.

On July 17, having been nine days in Yedo Bay, the fleet weighed anchor and went to sea. The *Saratoga* proceeded to Shanghai for the protection of American interests there, and the other vessels to Napa, where Perry arrived on the 25th. After renting a coaling depot of the islanders, he sailed for Hong Kong with the *Mississippi* and *Susquehanna*, leaving the *Plymouth,* Commander John Kelly, at Napa, under orders to visit the Coffin Islands and take possession of them in behalf of the United States. Kelly made the outward voyage to the islands in October, and on the 30th of that month took possession of them. at Newport,

Hillsborough Island, by hoisting the United States flag, firing a salute of seventeen guns, and burying a copper plate and a bottle.[25]

In the fall of 1853, the East India squadron was mainly occupied with the protection of American interests in China, which country was then suffering from a civil war. Several vessels had lately arrived from America, the steamship *Powhatan,* sloop of war *Vandalia,* corvette *Macedonian,* and storeships *Southampton* and *Lexington.* Two other vessels, the *Vermont* and *Alleghany,* which had been promised Perry, were detached from his command by the new government at Washington that came in with President Pierce. Perry directed the work of the squadron from Macao, where he established himself on shore, together with the artists and surveying officers of the expedition, who were employed in arranging and collating the scientific information that had been collected.

In November the French frigate *Constantine* suddenly left Macao under sealed orders; and about the same time a Russian squadron arrived at Shanghai, having lately visited Nagasaki where its commander had attempted to open negotiations with the Emperor. These movements aroused Perry's suspicions, and fearing that the French and Russians might interfere with his plans, he decided to act promptly by returning at once to Japan. In January, he assembled at Napa all the vessels of his fleet that could be spared from China. On February 1 the sailing ships *Macedonian,* Captain Joel Abbot, *Vandalia,* Commander John Pope, *Southampton,* Lieutenant J. J. Boyle, and *Lexington,* Lieutenant J. J. Glasson, sailed for Yedo Bay, and six days later they were followed by the steamers *Susquehanna,* Commander Franklin Buchanan, *Mississippi,* Commander S. S. Lee, and *Powhatan,* Commander W. J. McCluney. On the 11th the *Southampton* arrived at the "American anchorage," ten miles above Uraga; and two days later she was joined by the remaining vessels of the fleet.

Soon after Perry left Yedo Bay in July, 1853, copies of President Fillmore's letter to the Emperor were sent to many of the principal rulers and dignitaries of Japan, requesting them to express unreservedly their opinion of it; and more than forty of them did so. They were almost unanimous in opposition to the opening of their country permanently to foreign commerce. Several, however, were willing to try the experiment for a limited

[25] Log of the *Plymouth,* U. S. Navy Department Archives, Oct. 30, 1853.

period. Declaring that "the policy of the barbarians is first to enter a country for trade, then to introduce their religion, and afterward to stir up strife and contention," the prince of Mito memorialized his government in favor of war. In the end, the Emperor decided to conciliate the Americans by granting them their less important demands, and at the same time to prepare his country for defense. New forts were constructed along the coast, numerous cannon and bombs were cast, and three hundred thousand patriots repaired to Yedo.[26]

Soon after the *Susquehanna* arrived at the American anchorage, some Japanese officers came alongside her with a message from the Emperor. They were referred to Perry's representative, Commander Adams, who they informed that the Emperor had given orders to receive the fleet in a most friendly manner, that he had appointed five commissioners of high distinction to meet Perry and consider with him the propositions contained in the President's letter, and that a town called Kamakura, about twenty miles below Uraga had been designated as the place of meeting. This news was highly satisfactory to Perry, with the exception of that respecting the meeting place, to which he strongly objected. On learning of his objections, the Japanese proposed Uraga, where they had already begun to erect a council-house. This proposal Perry also rejected, urging the inconvenience of Uraga and its unsafety as an anchorage for his ships. For more than a week the question of a meeting place was discussed, neither side being willing to yield to the other. Finally, to expedite a settlement, Perry sailed up the bay with his fleet within sight of Yedo and within hearing of its bells. Soon after this movement was effected, the Japanese, fearing that the Americans intended to visit Yedo, proposed that the meeting be held on the beach near Yokohama. As this place was quite suitable and convenient, Perry accepted it. Here the Japanese erected a council-house, and Perry moored his ships near by, covering with his guns the shore for a distance of five miles.

The president of the Japanese commission was Hayashi, prince counsellor, and chief professor of the Chinese language and literature at the Great University of Japan, a profound scholar and dignified gentleman. Three of the other four members had the rank of "princes." By March 8 the commissioners and Perry

[26] Nitobe, I. O. The Intercourse between the United States and Japan 48-51.

had completed their preparations for the meeting. The second landing of the Americans was marked by even greater pageantry than the first. As this feature is not especially dwelt upon by Perry in his official account, from which the following extract is taken, it may be passed over without further notice:

At 11.30 a. m. on the day appointed, the escort, consisting of about five hundred officers, seamen, and marines, fully armed, embarked in twenty-seven barges, in command of Commander Buchanan, and, forming a line abreast, pulled in good order to the shore. The escort having landed and drawn up, I followed in my barge under an appropriate salute, and landing, was received by the escort and a party of Japanese officials, and conducted to the hall prepared for the conference, where I found in waiting the five commissioners, and was invited to be seated opposite the chief personage.

At this moment salutes were fired from the howitzers mounted in the launches, of twenty-one guns in honor of the Emperor, and seventeen for the Japanese commissioners. This display in landing was made altogether for purposes of policy, in accordance with the reasons already assigned.

After suitable interchanges of courtesy, I was requested to retire, with my suite, to an inner apartment, where the necessary business could be conducted undisturbed. Accordingly, accompanied by the captain of the fleet, the two interpreters, and my secretary, I withdrew with the commissioners to an adjoining room, separated from the principal hall by a flag suspended across the entrance. Refreshments having been served, a reply to the letter of the President presented in July last was handed to me and translated from the Dutch by Mr. Portman, and I replied to it verbally. I then handed to the chief commissioner a draught of a treaty, which I had previously prepared as the basis of one which I was desirous of negotiating with the Imperial government. This was accompanied by three other papers—one being a reply to the communication of the chief commissioner addressed to me from Uraga . . . ; another, a statement of my views with respect to the policy of bringing about a mutually advantageous compact between the United States and Japan . . . ; and the third, a memorandum . . . in further explanation of the motives which would govern me in conducting the negotiations, and asking for certain relaxations of the Japanese laws with respect to the squadron.[27]

On the conclusion of these preliminaries, the commodore informed the commissioners that a marine had recently died on board the *Mississippi,* and that he wished to bury his body at some suitable place on shore. The commissioners replied that the body would have to be taken to Nagasaki for burial. Perry raised objections to this disposition of it, proposing that it be interred on Webster Island, near the American anchorage. The commissioners strongly opposed this suggestion, but finally consented to permit the interment to take place at a spot adjoining

[27] Sen. Ex. Doc., No. 34, 33 Cong., 2 sess., pp. 125-126.

one of the temples in Yokohama. Perry was somewhat disappointed at the turn taken by the incident as he had hoped to acquire an interest in Webster Island with a view to subserving " some ulterior objects." On fixing the burial place of the marine, the first conference came to an end.

The Emperor's answer to the President's letter disclosed that he was willing to concede much respecting the relief of distressed mariners and the establishment of ports of resort, but that he was unwilling to open Japan for purposes of trade. At first Perry urged the commissioners to negotiate with him a treaty granting the United States the rights of commerce, threatening them with the possibility that his government would send out more ships and men " with instructions of more stringent import." He soon discovered, however, that it was impossible to obtain a concession of commercial privileges, and he therefore turned his attention to procuring favorable terms respecting the points conceded. The Japanese were willing to open two ports of resort for American ships, Nagasaki immediately, and one other port after five years. Perry obtained the substitution of Shimoda, a more convenient port, for Nagasaki, the designation of Hakodate as the second port, and the reduction of the interval preceding the opening of the second port to one year. He also obtained a provision granting shipwrecked sailors temporarily living at the two ports of resort considerable freedom of movement and complete immunity from such restrictions as the Dutch and Chinese were subjected to at Nagasaki, and he secured the concession to the United States of all privileges that should be subsequently granted to other nations. At his suggestion the right of sending an American consul to reside in Shimoda was granted.

Several conferences were held at the council-house near Yokohama before the treaty was completed on March 31, when it was signed by Perry and the commissioners. During the negotiations the Japanese and their visitors showed each other many courtesies. Presents were both given and received by them. Among those presented by Perry to the Japanese were a collection of rifles, muskets, swords, pistols and carbines, a cask of wine, one hundred gallons of whisky, several baskets of champagne, a box of perfumery, a telescope, two telegraphic instruments, three life-boats, one locomotive with tender, passenger car, and rails, four volumes of Audubon's Birds of America, eight baskets of Irish potatoes, and numerous agricultural implements. The natives were much interested in the locomotive and telegraphic apparatus, which were set up on shore and operated for their instruction. The gifts presented by the Japanese included two bundles of rice, three hundred chickens, gold lacquered writing implements, paper boxes, and book cases, some pieces of pongee, crape and silk, twenty umbrellas and thirteen dolls.

Perry dined the commissioners and their retinues on board the *Powhatan*, receiving them with all the honors and attentions due to persons of high rank. The fleet displayed the Japanese flag, the first time this emblem ever floated from the mast-head of foreign ships of war. In accordance with the Japanese custom, the subordinates were not seated with their superiors. A table for the commissioners, Perry and his captains was spread in the cabin, while the lesser notables dined on the quarter-deck. The visitors did full justice to the American viands, and having eaten to satiety, they after the manner of their country wrapped up and took with them the remnants of the feast. One of the commissioners fancied a large cake and was presented with it by the commodore, together with some cordial. Under the mellowing influence of the American wines and liquors, the visitors became exceedingly social, and a few even hilarious. The friendship of Nippon and America was frequently toasted, and many sentiments of mutual good will were expressed by host and guest.

On the fourth day after the treaty was signed, Commander H. A. Adams was dispatched to Washington with a copy of it, taking passage on board the *Saratoga* for San Francisco. Perry's work in Yedo Bay was practically completed. Before leaving, however, he got his fleet under way and approached near enough to Yedo to ascertain that it could be destroyed by a few light-draft steamers carrying guns of the heaviest calibers. On April 18, the slower vessels having already sailed, Perry with the *Powhatan* and *Mississippi* left the scene of his great achievement and proceeded to Shimoda. Thence he visited Hakodate, and from that place returned to Shimoda. The harbors of these ports were surveyed, friendly relations were established with the local governments, and cemeteries for the burial of Americans were located. At Shimoda the commodore met the Japanese commissioners and together they adopted some new treaty regulations, relating in part to the limits near the two ports within which the Americans were to be free to go and come, the landing places for vessels, and the sale of goods. Finally on June 28 Perry sailed for China by way of the Lu-chu Islands. At Napa he entered into a compact with the government, granting to Americans the same rights in the Lu-chus that the treaty of Yokohama gave them in Japan. On July 21 he arrived at Hong Kong.

For some time the commodore had been unwell, suffering from bodily ailments and worn out by the cares and duties of his trying office. In December, 1853, he had written to the Secretary of the Navy asking permission to return home when his negotiations with Japan should be completed. At Hong Kong he received the orders he had requested, and on September 11 he sailed from that port on the British mail steamer *Hindostan* for England by way of the Red Sea and the overland route. On January 11, 1855, he arrived in New York on the steamer *Baltic,* having been absent from the United States two years and two months. His flagship *Mississippi,* returning home by way of the west coast of South America, reached New York on April 22, and on the following day she was visited by Perry. As he left her to go ashore his broad pennant was hauled down, thus formally terminating his connection with the East India squadron.

The opening of Japan was a memorable achievement, whether viewed as an international spectacle, a difficult task, or an historical event. Its spectacular features arrested the attention and kindled the imagination of the whole civilized world. The surmounting of its difficulties might well have challenged the ablest statesmen of the century. Perry's success was in no small measure the result of a rare combination of strong qualities of character— firmness, sagacity, tact, dignity, patience and determination. The opening of Japan was one of the great historical events of the last century, the farreaching effects of which are still but partially revealed.

For several months after Perry's return to the United States, he was employed at Washington in preparing a history of his expedition. In 1856 this was published by the federal government in three large volumes at a total cost of three hundred and sixty thousand dollars.[28] On the completion of his labors as author and editor, he returned to his home in New York City, where he died after a brief illness on March 4, 1858.

[28] Griffis, W. E., Matthew Calbraith Perry, 385.

XIII

The East Indies Squadron, *1854-1865* [1]

The commanders-in-chief of the East India squadron, their periods of service, and their flagships, from the departure of Perry for the United States in 1854 to the discontinuance of the squadron on the outbreak of the Civil War in 1861, were as follows: Commodore Joel Abbot, 1854-1855, *Macedonian;* Commodore John Pope, 1855-1856, *Macedonian;* Commodore James Armstrong, 1856-1858, *San Jacinto;* Commodore Josiah Tattnall, 1858-1859, *San Jacinto* and *Powhatan;* Commodore C. K. Stribling, 1859-1861, *Hartford;* and Commodore Frederick Engle, 1861, *Hartford.* All of these officers, with the exception of Pope, who entered the navy in 1816, served in the War of 1812. Abbot died on the China station. Resigning from the federal navy in 1861, Tattnall was made senior flag officer of the Georgia navy and later captain in the Confederate navy, in which service he held several important commands. Armstrong was given no active duties at sea after 1858, nor Pope and Engle after 1861. In 1864-1865 Stribling commanded the East Gulf blockading

[1] The chief sources of information for this chapter are the East India Squadron Letters, 1853-1861; Commanders' Letters, November, 1861-March, 1862, July, 1863-January, 1864; Officers' Letters, February-April, 1862; Captains' Letters, February-September, 1864; Hoppin, J. M., Life of Andrew Hull Foote, 111-135; Jones, C. C., The Life and Services of Commodore Josiah Tattnall, 74-123; Johnston, J. D., China and Japan, 68-361; Williams, F. W., The Life and Letters of S. Wells Williams, 249-326; and Sen. Ex. Doc., No. 30, 36 Cong., 1 sess.

squadron. Armstrong and Pope reached the rank of commodore; and Engle and Stribling, of rear-admiral, on the retired list, the last named dying in 1880 the senior officer of his grade.

The East India squadron regularly consisted of three or four vessels until the outbreak of the Civil War, when its size was reduced and the squadron organization discontinued. When Pope took command of it in 1854, the principal ports visited by its ships were Canton, Whampoa, Macao, Hong Kong, Amoy, Ning-po, Fu-chau, Shanghai, Shimoda, Hakodate, Manila, and Singapore. Its headquarters were at Hong Kong, where in 1854 Perry established a naval depot, discontinuing the one at Macao. News from Europe and the United States was first received in China at Hong Kong, much of it coming by way of England and the overland route. In 1852, a naval depot was established at Shanghai, the American trade with which port three years later exceeded that with Canton. Our commerce with China was greatest from 1850 to 1860, declining rapidly during the Civil War and never regaining its former position after that conflict. By 1876 the British had driven the American ships entirely from the China trade, and were even supplying New York with early teas.

The period 1854-1865 in China was mainly one of civil strife and foreign wars, and consequently the officers of the American squadron were frequently called upon to protect the lives and property of their fellow-countrymen. The Taiping Rebellion, beginning in 1850 and lasting until 1865, was one of the greatest insurrections in the world's history, during which, it is said twenty million people lost their lives. The second English war with China began in 1856, and continued, with intermissions, for four years, France being drawn into the struggle in 1857. In 1863-1864 there was a revolution in Japan. The negotiating of a second American treaty with Japan in 1856-1857 and with China in 1858 gave additional work to the officers of the squadron.

In 1853-1854 the Taiping Rebellion caused Commodore Perry no little trouble, compelling him to station vessels in the neighborhood of both Canton and Shanghai. On March 6 of the latter year the Chinese war ship *Sir Herbert Compton,* fired upon an American pilot boat near Shanghai, brought her to, boarded her, hauled down her flag, captured her Chinese crew, and hung them up by their queues to the mainmast of the war ship. When Com-

mander John Kelly, of the U. S. ship *Plymouth,* received news of
this outrage, he ordered Lieutenant John Guest to proceed with
one of the cutters of the *Plymouth* to the *Sir Herbert Compton*
and obtain the release of the captured boat. Guest executed his
commission with such boldness and celerity that he retook the
prisoners and the boat without the firing of a shot on either side.
In April, Kelly co-operated with a party of British bluejackets
and volunteers in defending the lives and property of the
foreigners at Shanghai. The American party consisted of sixty
seamen and marines from the *Plymouth* and some thirty or forty
officers and sailors of merchantmen and residents of Shanghai.
The combined force attacked an encampment of Imperialists,
forcing it to retreat and leave its dead and wounded on the field.
The Americans lost one seaman killed and one seaman and two
marines wounded, and one merchant captain killed and the chief
clerk of the house of Russell and Company wounded.

In the fall of 1854, the chief seat of disturbance on the coast
of China was at Canton, which city then seemed likely to fall into
the hands of the Revolutionists, who had already taken Shanghai
and Amoy. For the protection of American interests, Commodore
Abbot stationed his flagship at Whampoa and the chartered
steamer *Queen* at Canton, and concerted measures of defense with
Rear-Admiral Sir James Stirling, the British commander-in-chief
in China. Determined to maintain a neutral position, Abbot came
into collision with some of the American residents at Canton, who
were in favor of preventing the Revolutionists from attacking the
city. When in March, 1855, the Imperialists defeated the Revolutionists, the civil commotion subsided, and Abbot dropped down
to Hong Kong.

The unsettled state of China was taken advantage of by pirates
who infested the entire coast of that country. In November, 1854,
a party of Americans under the command of Lieutenant G. H.
Preble, in co-operation with the British forces, struck a severe
blow at these freebooters, destroying sixty-eight of their junks
and two piratical depots situated on shore not far from Hong
Kong. One American seaman, belonging to a landing party commanded by Acting Master J. G. Sproston, was killed. Preble was
commended by both Commodore Abbot and Rear-Admiral Stirling. In the summer of 1855 he was again engaged in suppressing
the pirates, making two expeditions against them, one to the

southward and the other·to the northward of Shanghai. In the latter he again co-operated with the British visiting among other ports Chi-fu and Wei-hai-wei, where the American flag was displayed for the first time. In August of that year a party of seamen and marines from the American ship *Powhatan* and the English sloop *Rattler,* destroyed a fleet of piratical junks and captured many prisoners off Khulan. Nine seamen and marines were killed, five of whom were Americans. To commemorate this event a monument was erected in the cemetery at Happy Valley, Hong Kong.[2]

While Abbot was commander-in-chief of the squadron, but a single vessel, the steamer *Powhatan,* Captain W. J. McCluney visited Japan. She was dispatched thither with Commander H. A. Adams, the bearer of the ratified treaty of Yokohama, who had been ordered by the government at Washington to exchange ratifications with the Japanese. This formality took place at Shimoda on February 21, 1855, the *Powhatan* displaying a Japanese flag and firing a salute of seventeen guns. About a month before her arrival at Shimoda, an earthquake had greatly damaged that town and the neighboring region, injuring the Russian ship of war, *Diana,* Admiral E. Pontiatine, which sank at sea. Fortunately her officers and crew were rescued, and, being in distress, were generously supplied with provisions by McCluney. Pontiatine succeeded in his mission to Japan, the negotiation of a treaty similar to that of Perry.

The personnel of Commodore Abbot's squadron suffered more or less from severe diseases formerly so common on shipboard in the East Indies. That the commodore himself was stricken with a dire malady, we learn for the first time from a letter to the Secretary of the Navy, dated Hong Kong, November 12, 1855, in which he wrote incidentally as follows: " My own health is such that my fleet surgeon offers me no encouragement that I shall live to return to the United States, but remarks, however, if I could sail immediately, there might be some slight chance of my restoration to health, and I am strongly urged by many persons to do so ; but I belong to the old school and have been taught not ·to leave my post until regularly relieved." [3] A month later he

[2] Collum, R. S., History of the United States Marine Corps, 104; Ford J. D., An American Cruiser in the East, 405.

[3] East India Squadron Letters, 1854-1855, 279.

wrote his last dispatch to the department, and on the following day he died, at the residence of the naval storekeeper at Hong Kong. A few days later his body was removed to the *Macedonian,* under an escort of soldiers from Her Majesty's 59th Regiment, furnished by the governor of Hong Kong, and of marines from the English squadron, furnished by Rear-Admiral Stirling. During the march of the procession minute guns were fired by the *Macedonian,* the British frigate *Winchester,* and the British batteries on shore. From Hong Kong his body was trans- ported to America.

The officer next in rank was Captain John Pope, who at the time of Abbot's death was at Amoy in command of the *Vandalia.* Proceeding to Hong Kong, he transferred his flag to the *Macedonian,* and thence shortly sailed for Singapore, where on April 5 he was relieved by his successor in command of the squadron, Commodore James Armstrong, who had recently arrived there on board the flagship *San Jacinto,* Captain H. H. Bell. Continuing his voyage homeward, Pope reached Boston in August.

In the summer of 1856 Armstrong conveyed to Shimoda Mr. Townsend Harris, the first American consul-general to Japan. Here he spent two weeks awaiting the recognition of Harris by the Japanese government and Harris's removal ashore to the con- sular residence. Armstrong attended an entertainment given in honor of the Americans by the Imperial commissioners from Yedo, and he returned their courtesy by receiving them and their suites on board the *San Jacinto.* They were much pleased with the salute fired in their honor and with the exercises of the crew with the great guns and small arms. At one of the entertainments, they asked Armstrong if he could not take the consul-general away with him. " No," he replied, " my instructions are to take him to Shimoda, to see him established in his consular house, to erect his flagstaff, and to leave him there." They then asked if he could not convey to his government the reasons why they wished the consul-general to leave Shimoda; and he answered them that all communications to his government must be sent through Harris. To their third and last question, " At what time shall you leave ? " Armstrong curtly replied, " I shall leave when I am ready." [4]

From Shimoda the commodore went to Shanghai, where he arrived on September 13 ; and thence early in November, he sailed

---

[4] East India Squadron Letters, 1855-1856, 82-85.

for Hong Kong, giving passage to Dr. Peter Parker, the American commissioner to China. The American legation at this time was somewhat peripatetic, and was to be frequently found on board one of the ships of the squadron in transit from one Chinese port to another. When, as sometimes happened, it was denied transportation by the commander-in-chief, for what seemed to him good and sufficient reasons, the commissioner complained to the state department. Friction between the naval and diplomatic services in the Far East continued to exist until the government at Washington fixed definitely their respective spheres of duty.

While Armstrong was at Shanghai in October, 1856, hostilities broke out in the neighborhood of Canton between the English and Chinese. Mr. O. H. Perry, our consul at Canton, appealed to Commander A. H. Foote, of the ship *Portsmouth,* lying at Whampoa, to protect the lives and property of his fellow-countrymen. Foote responded by conveying to the American factory at Canton four boat loads of seamen and marines, eighty-one in number, which he organized into companies, posting sentinels on the house tops and manning some newly erected fortifications. He was shortly re-enforced by sixty-nine officers and seamen from the *Levant,* Commander W. Smith, which ship joined the *Portsmouth* at Whampoa. On November 3 some of Foote's sentinels were fired upon by Chinese soldiers and they returned the fire, but no one was injured.

Receiving information of Foote's movements, Armstrong sailed from Hong Kong to Whampoa, where he arrived in the *San Jacinto* on November 12, and at once dispatched the marine guard of his ship with arms and ammunition ʸo Canton. Three days later, after a consultation with Foote, he resolved, in order to avoid the danger of compromising our neutrality, to withdraw the forces that had been landed at Canton, a step urged by Yeh, the Chinese high commissioner and governor-general. He decided, however, to keep one of the vessels of the squadron near the factories as a refuge for the Americans in case their lives were endangered. On the afternoon of the 15th Foote left Whampoa for Canton for the purpose of directing Commander Smith to return to Whampoa and bring his ship up the river, preparatory to the withdrawal of the American forces from the city. For the events immediately succeeding Foote's departure, the official report of Armstrong may be quoted:

At about 5 p. m., Commander Foote returned to this ship and reported to me that, when off the forts, known as the " Barrier Forts," situated about midway betwen this anchorage (Whampoa) and Canton, his boat was fired into five times with both grape and round shot, but fortunately without doing any injury. I immediately dispatched Commanders Foote and Bell to procure one or more steamers for the purpose of towing the *Portsmouth* and *Levant* off those forts to redress this outrage upon our flag. At daylight the next morning (the 16th) the American steamer *Kum Fa* was dispatched by me to Canton to bring the marines, men, launches, and howitzers, belonging to this ship and to the *Portsmouth* down to the latter vessel. Lieutenant Williamson, of this ship, with one of our cutters, with an armed crew, and having with him Mr. Ayres, a pilot, was sent to sound out the channel up to the forts. Lieutenant Williamson returned to the ship at noon and reported that he had sounded to within less than half a mile of the forts, when he was fired upon three times with grape and round shot, and, I regret to say, that by one of the shots, the coxswain of the boat, Edward Mullen, was instantly killed, while in the act of heaving the lead.

The *Kum Fa* having returned to this anchorage with the force from Canton, I ordered Commander Bell to take command of the *Levant* (Commander Smith with a small force having been left at Canton, for the protection of our citizens and their property) ; and, having divided the crew of this ship with the *Portsmouth* and *Levant*, excepting some 60 men with Lieutenant Williamson and the warrant and engineer officers to take care of her (she drawing too much water to go up the river), I repaired on board the *Portsmouth*, accompanied by the fleet surgeon, Dr. Wood, and my secretary, hoisted my pennant on board of her, and in tow of the American steamer *Willamette,* the *Kum Fa* towing the *Levant,* got under way and stood up the Whampoa channel, and anchored in the *Portsmouth* within 500 yards of the nearest fort, at about 4.20 p. m., and got the ship in position for shelling the forts. The forts opened a brisk and well directed fire upon her before she had come to an anchor, which was at once returned by her with a rapid discharge of shells, and which was kept up with little intermission until dark. The Chinese fired exceedingly well and hulled the *Portsmouth* six times, but doing no material injury to her. The *Levant's* position, she having grounded about one mile below us and out of range, did not permit of her joining in the attack. The largest of the forts, and the one nearest to us, was silenced early in the evening; and the fire of the others became very languid at the close of the action. The *Portsmouth,* I regret to say, had one of her marine guards very seriously wounded.

The coolness and skill of Commander Foote in taking the *Portsmouth* into action under fire of the enemy, together with the enthusiasm and discipline displayed by his officers and crew, excited my warmest admiration. Never before had I seen such precision of firing or more steadiness in battle. During the night the *Levant* was got off and placed in position, keeping her broadside sprung all the following day upon the forts.

On the 17th the *Portsmouth* having grounded in the narrow channel, the two ships remained inactive, except in getting out kedges, etc., to haul off by. While in this condition, and in some degree at a disadvantage, the forts did not resume firing. I, therefore believing that their disposition or means of hostility had terminated, thought this a favorable opportunity to obtain from the Imperial Commissioner at Canton an explanation of the cause of the attack upon our flag and a security that it should not be repeated. With this in view I returned to the *San Jacinto,* leaving Commander Foote in command, with orders to keep in position upon the forts, but not to fire unless assailed by them.[5]

On the 19th, learning that the Chinese were repairing and strengthening their defenses, Armstrong ordered Foote to prevent this and " to take such measures as his judgment would dictate, if it were even the capture of the forts." How thoroughly Foote carried out his orders may be seen from his official report, dated November 26, 1856.

At 6.30, on the morning of the 20th instant, both ships being in position and in all respects ready for action, we beat to quarters, and simultaneously opened on the two nearest forts. After an interval of five minutes the fire was briskly returned until 7.45, when it materially slackened. The storming party, consisting of 287 persons—officers, seamen and marines—with four howitzers, commanded by myself—Commanders Bell and Smith leading respectively detachments from the *San Jacinto* and *Levant*—then left the ships, and pulled in three columns for the shore. The company of marines was most efficiently led by Captain [John D.] Simms. While landing, Louis Hetzel and Thomas Krouse (apprentice boys) were killed by the accidental discharge of a Minie rifle. The party formed, and marched towards the fort, dragging three howitzers with them across the rice-fields, and wading a creek waist deep. In order to attack the fort in the rear it was necessary to pass through a village, in which several shots were fired upon us, till the howitzers cleared the streets, and secured for us an unobstructed advance. When near the fort, the soldiers were seen fleeing from it, many of them swimming for the opposite shore. The marines, being in advance, opened fire upon the fugitives with deadly effect, killing some 40 or 50. The American flag was planted on the walls of the fort by a lieutenant from the *Portsmouth.* As the fort opposite was playing upon us with some energy, the guns we had captured—53 in number—were several of them brought to bear and soon silenced it, but not before a shot had struck the *Portsmouth's* launch in the water line and sunk her. She floated, however, at the flood, and was soon rendered efficient for further service. The city of Canton being only four miles distant, a portion of its army, variously estimated at from 5000 to 15,000, and which I believe to have numbered at least 3000, was stationed near. This force twice advanced; but they were both times repulsed by the marines, with 10 or 12 killed; and, as they were retreating, a deadly fire was opened upon them from one of the howitzers. During one of these skirmishes a man belonging to the *Portsmouth's* howitzer crew received a shot-wound in the

[5] East India Squadron Letters, 1855-1856, 125-127.

leg. While firing at the opposite fort, a boatswain's mate from the *Portsmouth* was wounded in the head and foot by the bursting of a gun. A small portion of the force was withdrawn at night, and the fort was occupied by the commander of the *San Jacinto* with the remaining force till morning.

At three a. m. the next day an 8-inch shot from one of the forts struck the *Portsmouth* and lodged in the bends. This was instantly returned by three of her shells, and the fort was at once silenced. At four a. m., the commander of the *San Jacinto*, with the force which had occupied the captured fort during the night, embarked and returned to the ship. At six o'clock both ships opened their fire on the three remaining forts, which was at first briskly returned. During the action Edward Riley (O. S.) was mortally wounded aboard the *Levant*, and died this evening. The fort nearest the ships having been silenced, at seven o'clock the boats in tow of the American steamer *Kum Fa*, temporarily in charge of Mr. Robinet, having on board the engineers from the *San Jacinto*, Mr. Henry C. Victor and Mr. C. H. Baker, with a crew from the *San Jacinto*, left the ships and proceeded towards the object of attack. While passing the barrier, a ricochet 64-pound shot from the farthest fort struck the boat abreast of my own, completely raking it, and instantly killing James Hoagland, carpenter's mate, and mortally wounding William Mackin and Alfred Turner, who died soon after. Seven others were also wounded more or less severely. The boat struck was the launch of the *San Jacinto*, in charge of the first lieutenant of that ship. The steamer stood in with the boats in tow, till they were covered by an intervening neck of land, on which the party landed. After wading a ditch waist deep, and receiving several shots from gingals and rockets, the fort was carried, with one of the marines severely wounded, in presence of a thousand or more Chinese soldiers just beyond howitzer range. A corporal of marines, the standard-bearer of the company, planted the American flag upon the walls. Several of the guns of the fort, with our howitzers, were brought to bear upon the center fort, commanding the river, which had opened fire upon us. It was soon silenced. The other guns, in the fort we had captured, which were altogether 41 in number, were spiked, their carriages burned, and everything destructible, by the means in our power, destroyed.

At four p. m. the marines advanced on the bank of the river and captured a breastwork mounting six guns; a party of Chinese soldiers, some hundreds in number, advanced towards them, but were soon repulsed by two companies of sailors, led by their lieutenants. In the meantime one of the howitzers played upon a still greater number, who were drawn up in front of and around a pagoda, until they were dispersed, and retreated carrying off their killed and wounded. The boats, under fire from the fort on the opposite side of the river, had been tracked up to the breastwork, and now, under cover of its guns and those of the fort just captured, they crossed with the party to the island, and took possession of its fort, containing 38 guns; one of these was a brass gun, of 8-inch calibre, and 22 feet five inches in length, greatest circumference eight feet three inches, diameter of bore eight and a half inches. The standard-bearer of marines was again the first to plant the American flag upon the walls. The same work of destruction as to the two forts previously captured was here renewed. The only fort remaining in the possession of the enemy on the Canton side of the river at once opened upon us. Accordingly the guns in the fort we occupied were brought to bear, and, with the assistance of the howitzers, silenced it in the course of half an hour. It now being dark it was thought expedient to suspend further operations till morning.[6]

On the following day a landing party captured the fourth and last fort of the enemy without the loss of a man, notwithstanding it had to face a brisk fire for some time. Foote's victory was most decisive. His loss was thirty-four men, while that of the enemy was about two hundred and fifty. The Chinese had one hundred and seventy-six guns, many of eight-inch calibre and larger, but they were unable to use them effectively. Forty-nine shots struck the hulls and rigging of the *Portsmouth* and *Levant,* but did little damage. Foote and his men fought with great skill and courage, and were warmly commended by Armstrong. The Secretary of the Navy approved the measures pursued by the Americans, declaring that the brave and energetic manner in which they had avenged the wrong committed by the Chinese was worthy of all praise, and that the gallantry, good order, and intelligent subordination of officers, sailors, and marines were highly creditable to the service. He however expressed an earnest anxiety to cultivate and maintain friendly relations with the people and government of China, adding that they must be taught to respect us, but that the lesson must be given with " generous forbearance and the studied avoidance of unnecessary collision." [7]

In the winter of 1856-1857 the commotion at Canton subsided, and the ships of the squadron were withdrawn from the Canton River. In the course of the year 1857 they visited most of the important ports of the East India station, including Shimoda and Hakodate, Japan, where in the fall the *Portsmouth,* Commander A. H. Foote, spent several weeks. The Japanese government was then manifesting a friendly feeling for Americans, partly as a result of the skillful diplomacy of Consul-General Harris, who had negotiated a convention with Japan, opening Nagasaki as a third port of resort. A few days after the arrival of the *Portsmouth* at Shimoda, Foote, accompanied by Harris and four of his wardroom officers, called upon the two governors stationed here. "We were received," wrote Foote in describing his visit, ' with great courtesy and apparent cordiality. They enquired with a good deal of interest how the President and Government of the United States regarded Japan; about the war in China, its cause and probable result; and expressed the hope that at some future period, the Japanese would visit America for the purposes of education and obtaining a knowledge of many things in which they acknowledged their deficiency. I stated to the governors that our men of war in future would no doubt visit Japan more frequently, as the occupation of the squadron in looking out for our interests in China had prevented a vessel being in Shimoda and Hakodate during the past year." [8]

On January 29, 1858, Commodore Armstrong transferred the squadron to his successor, Commodore Josiah Tattnall, and returned to the United States. Tattnall first hoisted his broad pennant on board the *San Jacinto,* but on the arrival at Hong Kong of the *Powhatan,* in May, he made that vessel his flagship. His most important work in the Far East was performed in connection with the negotiation of new treaties with China by the principal Occidental powers. In the spring of 1858 he placed at the service of Mr. William B. Reed, the American envoy, the steamers *Minnesota,* Commander S. F. Dupont, and *Mississippi,* Commander W. C. Nicholson, and chartered for his use from the house of Russell and Company, the light-draft steamer, *Antelope.* Reed's plan was to negotiate a treaty at or near Peking, which lies in the interior. near the Peiho, one of the largest rivers of northern China, emptying into the bay of Pechili. On arriving at the mouth of the Peiho, he, together with the envoys of Great Britain, France, and Russia, were delayed some time by the dilatory tactics of the Chinese. While waiting here, Commander Dupont conferred with Tan, one of the Chinese high commissioners, and delivered to him the official letter of President Buchanan. Finally, after the British and French fleets had opened the river by capturing the Taku forts near its mouth, Reed and Dupont proceeded to Tientsin, seventy miles distant, on board the *Antelope.* Here, on June 28, Reed and the Chinese commissioners signed the Treaty of Tientsin. On returning to the mouth of the Peiho he reported his success to Tattnall, who had arrived there

[8] East India Squadron Letters, 1857-1858, 214-215.

with the *Powhatan*. The negotiations of the British, French, and Russians were also successful. The new treaties with China provided for the opening of several additional ports to foreign commerce, granted to foreigners many important privilege respecting trade, property, and travel, and permitted representatives of the Western powers to reside at Peking.

On the ratification of the Treaty of Tientsin by the President and Senate, Mr. John E. Ward, Reed's successor, was directed to exchange ratifications with the Chinese government. Arriving at Penang, Ward was given passage on board the *Powhatan*, to Hong Kong. Here Tattnall purchased the English steamer *Toey wan*, a small vessel of one hundred and seventy-five tons burden for use in ascending the Peiho. Stopping at Shanghai, Ward conferred with the Chinese high commissioners, and at their request consented to proceed to Peking with the English and French envoys, who had been appointed by their respective governments to exchange ratifications. On June 21, 1859, the *Powhatan* and *Toey-wan* arrived at the anchorage off the mouth of the Peiho, where they found the fleets of Great Britain and France. Here the progress of the envoys was arrested by some newly erected forts and barricades. The commanders of the British and French fleets notified the Chinese that if they did not remove these obstacles by the 25th, the day fixed for the exchange of ratifications, they would do so themselves. The Chinese insisted that the true mouth of the Peiho was ten miles northward, and that the envoys should proceed thither and await the arrival of the commissioners from Shanghai. After deliberating over the situation, Tattnall and Ward decided to pretend ignorance of the fact that access had been denied the English and French, and to pass up the river as far as the barricades in the *Toey-wan*. Their movements are thus described by Tattnall in a letter written on July 4:

We entered the river in execution of our plan at 11 a. m on the 24th ult. and passing through the British squadron without communicating pushed up towards the barriers. At this time not a man was to be seen at the forts, nor a gun in an embrasure, nor, although flagstaffs were on the parapets, was a flag displayed. There was nothing to indicate that the forts were armed or manned. Subsequent events show this to have been a deception and ambuscade, intended, I do not doubt (in the confidence of their own strength and the small force of the English) to invite a conflict in order to annul the treaties of last year. We had approached to within three hundred yards of the first barrier, at which point should we not be fired on, I had purposed anchoring, when we grounded and failed in all our efforts to back off. The tide was falling fast and our situation was critical, not only from the facility with which the batteries might demolish us, but, as we were on the edge of a steep bank, from the probability of the steamer falling over and filling.

At this moment I received from Admiral James Hope an attention and kindness which must place me under lasting obligations to him. Although he had reason to think that she would be fired upon by the forts, he sent a gunboat to my aid, with the message that, had he known of my intention to pass up he would have furnished me a pilot, and that he expected to see me fired on. The gunboat failed in her effort to extricate me and there being, as I have said, a probability of the *Toey-wan's* falling over and filling, the Admiral despatched a second gunboat to me, placing her entirely at my disposition, with the handsome and generous offer that I should hoist on board of her the American ensign and my own personal flag. I declined the offer, with a just appreciation, however, of the personal kindness to myself and the delicate compliment to our service. The *Toey-wan* was more fortunate than I expected, and a favorable wind having sprung up we got her off at high water.

About two hours after grounding we sent a boat to the nearest fort with my flag lieutenant, Mr. Trenchard, and the interpreter to inform the commanding officer that the American minister was on board the *Toey-wan* on his way to Tientsin and Peking in accordance with our treaty and an understanding with the Chinese commissioners at Shanghai. They were met at the landing by an officer, professing to be of low rank, who said that his orders were, not to permit the removal of the barriers and to fire on those attempting it. That he believed that a high officer had been appointed to meet the ministers at the North. He also asserted most falsely, as subsequently shown, that there were no troops and only a few country militia in the forts. Although the interpreters were allowed to get out of the boat for greater facility of conversation, they were not permitted to approach the forts.[9]

On the afternoon of the 25th (to be exact, at 2.45 p. m.), the British and French, to the number of twelve hundred men, sailed up the river for the purpose of removing the obstructions. As they approached the first barrier, they were fired into by the Chinese forts, which suddenly became alive with soldiers, hitherto concealed. Taken thus by surprise, they were overwhelmingly defeated, losing four hundred and fifty men, killed and wounded. For a time Tattnall remained in the rear of the contestants, painfully disappointed at the turn the engagement had taken. For the part that he later played his own words are the best authority:

The fire was concentrated on the flag of the admiral. By this time, 4 p. m., several of his vessels had been sunk and it was evident to me that

[9] East India Squadron Letters, 1858-1859, 158-159.

nothing could enable him to extricate himself and retire from the hopeless conflict, but the reserve of boats and men at the junks; but at the time the tide was running too strong for the crowded boats to stem. The officer in charge of these boats now visited me. He said nothing of aid, but his silent appeal was powerful indeed. In the few moments he was on board he would look anxiously, alternately at his admiral and at the boats.

After he left I held a consultation with Mr. Ward, and he agreed with me perfectly that under all the circumstances of our position with the English, and the aid the admiral had tendered me the day before, I could do no less than to tow the boats to his relief. I made the offer which was thankfully and promptly accepted. While the boats were making fast to hawsers, which I veered astern, I insisted on Mr. Ward and his suite leaving the *Toey-wan* and going on board one of the junks, for reasons that will be obvious. He at first reluctantly yielded and left us, but soon returned in one of the English boats, declaring that, as the *Toey-wan* was his home and was going under fire with his approbation and concurrence, he would remain in her. I reluctantly yielded to his gallant impulse. At this time a young British officer came to me from the vessels engaged, to say that the gallant admiral was dangerously wounded, and had but six men left. He (the officer) had two boats sunk in reaching me. I towed the boats through the British line to within a short distance of the admiral, whose flag was flying on the *Cormorant,* when, casting them off, I retired to the rear of the line, near the French gun-boat and anchored for the night. I took up this position as it might enable me to aid the wounded, and, should boats be sunk, to rescue their crews.

After anchoring I thought of the admiral and of his chivalrous kindness to me the day before, which, from an unwillingness to intrude on him when he was preparing for action, I had in no way yet acknowledged. I, therefore, with my flag lieutenant, Mr. Trenchard, went in my barge to visit him. When within a few feet of the *Cormorant,* a round shot struck the boat, killed my coxswain and slightly bruised my flag lieutenant. We fortunately reached the *Cormorant* before the boat entirely filled. I found the admiral lying on his quarter-deck, badly wounded. I informed him that I had called to pay him my respects and to express my regret at his condition. After remaining on board the *Cormorant* about ten minutes I took advantage of an English boat that was passing to return to the *Toey-wan.*

The *Cormorant* after this was sunk and the admiral, shifted his flag to a fourth vessel, the *Coromandel* (a thing I believe unprecedented), thus evincing an indomitable valor under very disheartening and almost hopeless circumstances. At dusk, about 8 p. m., a desperate attempt was made, by landing from boats to storm the forts, but they stood in an impassable morass and the assailants were repelled with heavy loss.

On the morning following this day and night of slaughter, the action still continuing, but the fire more feeble and distant, I found that six of the English vessels were sunk, and that the remainder had withdrawn to a more distant and safer position, from which they could easily retire out of gunshot. I now prepared to return to the *Powhatan* with Mr. Ward, but first called on board the *Coromandel* to take leave of the admiral and also on board the French gunboat to enquire after the French Commodore, Tricault, whom I had met on board the *Cormorant* when I called on the admiral and who had subsequently been wounded. I deferred my departure, by request, that I might tow to their ships at sea two launch loads of the wounded English. On reaching the *Powhatan* I again despatched the *Toey-wan* into the harbor in charge of Lieutenant [James D.] Johnston (first of the *Powhatan*), with orders to remain at the mouth of the harbor, out of fire, and to afford all aid consistent with our neutrality. After an efficient performance of this duty for 24 hours he rejoined me.

The sea officers with me in the *Toey-wan* on this service were Captain [George F.] Pearson, Lieutenant [Stephen D.] Trenchard and [Alexander A.] Semmes, all of the *Powhatan,* and Midshipman [Clarke] Merchant of the *Germantown.* The engineer officers were Messrs. [George W.] City and [Edward R.] Archer. Captain A. S. Taylor of the marine corps was also with me. I have to thank them for their zealous services.[10]

Certain other aid rendered the British by the Americans is not mentioned by Tattnall in his official report. The injuries done to his boat by the Chinese on the occasion of his first visit to Admiral Hope caused it to fill, partly sink, and float away, compelling the crew to seek refuge on the *Cormorant.* Finding themselves aboard a British vessel during a fight, some of the men, following their own impulses, and being, as they expressed it, " in the way and nowhere to go," joined the weary Britishers at the guns and helped them to load. When the commodore returned to the *Toey-wan,* a few men were left behind, as they were too busy at the guns to hear his call, and remained with the British a good part of the night. None of them was wounded.[11]

Tattnall undoubtedly violated his country's neutrality. The grounds of his defense were that he was placed in a measure on the same footing as the English and French, since in response to a request of the Chinese the three envoys were acting in unison; and that, as Admiral Hope had aided him when in a precarious position, he could do nothing less than return the favor. It was in this connection that he so aptly quoted the ancient proverb, " Blood is thicker than water." The administration at Washington approved his conduct, and the government at London expressed its thanks to President Buchanan, requesting that they be communicated to him and to Ward. The generosity of the

[10] East India Squadron Letters, 1858-1859, 160-162.
[11] Williams, F. W., The Life and Letters of S. Wells Williams, 305; Clowes, W. L., The Royal Navy, VII, 128-129.

Americans was much appreciated by the officers of the Royal Navy, and they never forgot it. After the Civil War, Tattnall having taken the losing side in that conflict, some British officers subscribed a sum of money for the relief of his wants.

The repulse of the British and French fleets at the Taku forts caused them to return to Shanghai. The American fleet sailed northward to the mouth of the Pehtang river, ten miles from the Peiho, where friendly relations were established with the governor-general of Pechili. On July 20 Mr. Ward, Lieutenant Trenchard, and several other officers proceeded to Peking. After a short stay there, they returned, having failed to exchange ratifications, a formality that finally took place at the mouth of the Pehtang. On the completion of Ward's mission, the American ships sailed for Shanghai.

In the summer of 1858 Tattnall visited Nagasaki in the *Powhatan,* meeting there the *Mississippi*—the first American naval vessels to call at that port since the visit of the *Preble* in 1849. From Nagasaki he sailed for Shimoda, where he arrived in season to be of assistance to Consul-General Harris, who had recently made a treaty with Japan that was still unsigned. Fearing that one of the European nations might complete a treaty before the Americans completed theirs, he readily consented to convey Harris to Kanagawa and assist him in obtaining the desired signatures. On July 29 the new treaty between America and Japan was signed in the cabin of the *Powhatan*. It provided for the residence of diplomatic agents at Yedo, and of consuls at the open ports, the number of which was increased to six by the addition of Kanagawa, Niigata, and Hyogo.

About this time the Japanese decided to send an embassy to America, and, on the request of the government of Japan, Tattnall agreed to convey it thither on board a national vessel. He transferred the squadron to his successor at Hong Kong in November, 1859, and a few weeks later proceeded to Yedo Bay. On January 16, the ambassadors came on board the *Powhatan* to pay their respects and view their quarters, being received with a salute of seventeen guns. On February 13 Tattnall sailed for San Francisco, with a party of seventy-one Japanese, including Chief Ambassador Shimmi, an assistant ambassador, a censor, ten minor officials, two doctors, three interpreters, and an array of barbers, pike-bearers, armorers, and servants.[12]

[12] Griffis, W. E., Townsend Harris, 323.

The duties of the East India squadron under the command of Commodore C. K. Stribling were largely of a routine character. In October, 1860, Stribling in his flagship *Hartford,* on a voyage from Nagasaki to Kanagawa, passed through the Inner Sea of Japan, a channel which was that year opened for the first time to foreign ships.   Returning to Hong Kong, he was appointed chargé d'affairs to China *ad interim,* by Minister Ward, an office which he filled for several months.   On November 9, 1860, the steam frigate *Niagara,* arrived at Kanagawa, with the Japanese embassy, which was returning home from America.   When on the following day the distinguished passengers disembarked, the yards were manned and a salute was fired in their honor.

In the spring of 1861 there were five vessels on the East India station.   On March 18 of that year, the Secretary of the Navy ordered two of them to return home, and on the outbreak of the Civil War, he gave the three remaining vessels similar orders, and directed Commodore Stribling to transfer his squadron to Captain Frederick Engle, his senior officer, and to return to America by way of the overland route.   A few weeks before Stribling was superseded, he issued the following general order for the purpose of quieting the excitement in his fleet caused by the fall of Fort Sumter, and of arousing a sentiment in behalf of the Union among those who wavered in their allegiance.   That its author was a native of South Carolina makes it all the more remarkable.

The commander-in-chief feels called upon at this time to address those under his command upon the condition of our country.

By the last mail we have authentic accounts of the commencement of civil war in the United States, by the attack and capture of Fort Sumter by the forces of the Confederate States.

It is not my purpose to discuss the merits of the cause or causes which has resulted in plunging our country into all the horrors of a civil war, but to remind those under my command of their obligations now to a faithful and zealous performance of every duty.   Coming as we do from the various sections of the country, unanimity of opinion upon this subject cannot be expected, and I would urge upon all the necessity of abstaining from all angry and inflammatory language upon the causes of the present state of things in the United States, and to recollect that here we have nothing to do but perform the duty of our respective stations and to obey the orders of our superiors in authority; to this we are bound by the solemn obligations of our oath.

I charge all commanders and other officers to show in themselves a good example of virtue, honor, patriotism, and subordination; and to be vigilant in inspecting the conduct of all such as are placed under their command.

The honor of the nation, of the flag, under which many of us have served from boyhood, our own honor and good name, require us now, if ever, that we suffer no blot upon the character of our country while the flag of the Union is in our keeping.[13]

Soon after Engle took charge of the squadron in July, he sailed from Hong Kong for the United States with two of the three vessels under his command, leaving on the station only the *Saginaw*, Commander J. F. Schenck, which ship was too frail to make the homeward voyage at that season of the year. Eager to take part in the war, Schenck, in January, 1862, placed the *Saginaw* in ordinary, leaving her in charge of Lieutenant Charles J. McDougal, with an assistant engineer and six seamen, and embarking with the rest of his officers and crew on board the American merchantman *Swordfish*, bound for San Francisco. Schenck's desire to assist in putting down the rebellion did not excuse him to the department, which chose to consider his action as an abandonment of his vessel. In April, 1862, McDougal was ordered by the British government to remove the *Saginaw* from Hong Kong, since her presence there violated the Queen's neutrality. He proceeded to Macao with her, and thence in a few weeks sailed for San Francisco, where he arrived in July.

From the departure of the *Saginaw* until the arrival at Manila of the steamer *Wyoming*, Commander David McDougal, in August, 1862, there were no national ships in Eastern waters. The *Wyoming*, remained on the Chinese station until the spring of 1864. In June, 1863, she was joined by the corvette, *Jamestown*, Captain Cicero Price, who did not return home until the summer of 1865. Since, during the Civil War, the naval laurels were to be won in America, service in the Far East was not prized by our officers. Writing in December, 1862, to the department, Commander McDougal requested it to direct the return home of his ship in order that he and his officers might " share in the stirring events of the times."

In 1863-1864 the duties of the little fleet were enlivened by several rather important occurrences. In the fall of the former year news reached China that the Confederate cruiser, *Alabama*, was expected in the East Indies, and McDougal at once sailed thence in search of her. Here he cruised for several months, led hither

[13] East India Squadron Letters, 1859-1861, 255.

and thither by rumor and conjecture but never catching sight
of the elusive rover, although at one time, when she was passing
through the Straits of Sunda, within twenty-five miles of her. At
Singapore, a half hour after his arrival, he was presented with
the British proclamation of neutrality requiring him to leave
within twenty-four hours. In marked contrast was his treatment
by the Dutch officers at Batavia and Rhio, who expressed " strong
friendship and sympathy for our cause and country." At the
latter place the Dutch government lent him some of its coal.
Several times the British authorities gave him trouble, alleging
that he violated the laws of neutrality and the customs of courtesy.

Captain Price also searched for the *Alabama.* On hearing
rumors that she would probably dock in some Chinese port, he
went to Amoy in quest of her, and thence sailed to the East Indies,
but failed to find her, as she had before his arrival left that
quarter for British India. In the spring of 1865 rumors were circulated in the Far East that the Confederate cruiser, *Shenandoah,*
had appeared in the China seas, but these proved to be false, and
the fears of the American residents in China and Japan were
allayed.

The protection of American interests in Japan was the most
important service rendered by the *Wyoming* and *Jamestown.*
About 1863 the balance of power in that country shifted from the
Shogun at Yedo (the Emperor of Perry and early American
visitors) to the Mikado, at Kyoto (the real Emperor).   The
ascendency of the Mikado's party was accompanied with demon-
strations against foreign residents. In May, 1863, the American
legation at Yedo was burned, and our minister Mr. R. H. Pruyn,
was forced to retire to Yokohama.   In June the American
merchant steamer, *Pembroke,* when on a voyage from Yokohama
to Shanghai, was fired on near Shimonoseki at the western entrance
to the Inland Sea, by some vessels of the Prince of Nagato, one
of the leaders of the anti-foreign agitation. McDougal was at
Yokohama when he heard of this outrage, and he at once proceeded to the scene of it with the *Wyoming.* For the events after
his arrival there, his official report may be quoted:

On the tide proving favorable we proceeded in the straits, and on opening the town of Shimonoseki discovered a steamer, brig, and bark of war
at anchor off the town, with Japanese colors at the peak and the flag of
the prince at the fore. We stood for the vessels and on approaching were
fired on as we got in range by six batteries, on different positions, mount-

ing from two to four guns each. Passing betwen the brig and bark on the
starboard hand and the steamer on the port, we received and returned
their fire at pistol shot; rounding the bow of the steamer and getting in
position, maintained the action for about one hour. During the affair the
steamer got under way, but two well directed shells exploded her boilers.
The brig appeared to be settling by the stern and no doubt sank. The
amount of damage done the bark must have been serious, as well as great
destruction on shore. The straits, opposite the city, are about three-fourths
of a mile wide, with strong currents, which made it very difficult to
maneuver the ship properly. As I had no charts and my pilots completely
paralyzed and apprehensive of getting on shore (in fact did touch once),
I was induced to withdraw out of action.

The fire from the shore battery was extremely brisk and continued so
as long as we were in range. We were hulled 11 times, and with considerable damage to smoke-stack and the rigging aloft, which was attributed to our passing within the range they were prepared for. I regret
to state the loss of four killed and seven wounded (one of whom since
dead). . . . It affords me much pleasure to state that the conduct of the
officers and crew was all I could desire.[14]

Soon after this engagement, McDougal returned to Yokohama,
where he remained several weeks before sailing for China. On
his departure the care of American interests in Japan fell entirely
to Captain Price of the *Jamestown,* who posted a marine guard
at the American legation, and who joined the English, French,
Dutch, and Prussians, in the establishment of a military patrol for
the security of the foreigners residing in Yokohama. When in the
summer of 1864, the American minister visited Yedo, Price gave
him passage on the *Jamestown,* escorted him to his residence, and
provided him with a guard of sixty men. In July of that year the
Prince of Nagato, who was determined to prevent foreigners from
navigating the Inland Sea, fired into the American steamer
Monitor, an irresponsible rover that had been knocking about
in the ports of Japan for a year or more. As the English, French,
and Dutch had suffered similar indignities at the hands of the
prince, they united with the Americans to chastise the offender
and to maintain by force of arms the rights guaranteed them by
treaty. An expedition, consisting of eighteen ships and a landing
force of about eleven hundred men, was prepared and sent to
Shimonoseki. Since the *Jamestown* was not adapted for service
in shallow waters, Price rented the little steamer *Takiang,* and
placed Ensign Frederick Pearson in command of her, with orders
to join the expedition. Hostilities began on September 5 and

lasted five days, at the end of which time all the forts and batteries of the enemy had been destroyed, with a loss to the allies of twelve killed and sixty wounded. The *Takiang's* share in the operations consisted in the towing of boats within range of the enemy, the firing of a few shots from a Parrott gun, and the taking care of the wounded. As the result of the victory, the Inland Sea was again opened to foreigners, the prince was pacified, and the allies demanded an indemnity of three million dollars.

In 1864 Price erected a naval hospital at Yokohama on a lot reserved for the use of the United States government. As his presence near the capital gave moral support to the Shogun, who was favorably disposed toward foreigners, he remained at Yokohama the larger part of a year. He left Japan for China in April, 1865, and on June 17 sailed from Macao for San Francisco.

XIV

Explorations, Surveys, and Missions, *1888-1857*[15]

The first exploring expedition sent out by the American government, sailed from Norfolk for the South Sea in August, 1838. It was commanded by Lieutenant Charles Wilkes, who is now chiefly remembered as the captor of Mason and Slidell at the beginning of the Civil War; and it contained six vessels: the flagship, *Vincennes,* brig *Porpoise,* ships *Peacock* and *Relief,* and schooners *Flying Fish* and *Sea Gull.* Its main objects were the survey and exploration of the South Sea, the discovery of islands, reefs, and shoals, and the ascertaining of their true position, and the acquiring of scientific information. A corp of scientists, learned in philology, biology, mineralogy, conchology, botany, and horticulture accompanied the expedition. Among them was the biologist Charles Pickering, the geologist James D. Dana, and the ethnologist Horatio Hale. The work in astronomy, hydrography, geography, magnetism, meteorology, and physics was entrusted to officers of the navy. With Wilkes's explorations in Samoa, the Feejee and Friendly Islands, Australia, New Zealand, the Antarctic region, the West coast of America, and Hawaii, we are not here concerned. Respecting his duties in the East Indies and the Far East, Secretary of the Navy, Paulding, gave him the following instructions, having previously referred to the exploration of our Northwest Coast:

[15] For sources of information, see the Wilkes Exploring Expedition, U. S. Navy Department Archives, Vol. II; Wilkes, C., Narrative of the United States Exploring Expedition, V, 275-410; East India Squadron Letters, 1848-1850, 286-293; 1857-1858, 253; Ringgold-Rodgers Surveying Expedition, U. S. Navy Department Archives; Habersham, A. W., My Last Cruise; and Wood, W. M., Fankwei, 149-260.

You will then proceed to the coast of Japan, taking in your route as many doubtful islands as possible, and you have permission to pass through the Straits of Sangar into the Sea of Japan, where you may spend as much time as is compatible with your arrival at the proper season in the Sea of Sooloo or Mindoro. Of this sea you will make a particular examination, with a view to ascertain whether there is any safe route through it which will shorten the passage of our vessels to and from China. It is enjoined on you to pay very particular attention to this object, in order that you may be enabled to furnish sailing instructions to navigators. It may be also advisable to ascertain the disposition of the inhabitants of the islands of this archipelago for commerce, their productions and resources.

Having completed this survey, you will proceed to the Straits of Sunda, pass through the Strait of Billeton, which you will examine, and thence to the port of Singapore.[16]

On November 27, 1841, Wilkes left the Hawaiian Islands for the East Indies. Owing to the lateness of the season and the loss of one of his vessels, he abandoned the proposed visit to Japan. The carrying out of the orders of the department respecting the Philippines fell to the *Vincennes* and the *Flying Fish,* which vessels arrived at Manila on January 3, 1842. Here he remained eight days, studying the customs of the people and acquiring information respecting the history, government, and geography of the islands. A scientific party, of which Dana and Pickering were members, explored the interior of Luzon. Soon after his arrival at Manila, Wilkes, accompanied by Mr. Moore, the American vice consul, made an official call on the governor of the Philippines, Don Marcelino Oroa. Of his reception by that official, he wrote as follows:

On our arrival, we were announced, and led up a flight of steps, ample and spacious, but by no means of such splendor as would indicate the residence of vice-royalty. The suite of rooms into which we were ushered were so dark that it was difficult to see. I made out, however, that they were panelled, and by no means richly furnished. His excellency entered from a side door, and led us through two or three apartments into his private audience room, an apartment not quite so dark as those we had come from; our being conducted to this, I was told afterwards, was to be considered an especial mark of respect to my country. His reception of us was friendly. The governor has much more the appearance of an Irishman than of a Spaniard, being tall, portly, of a florid complexion. He is apparently more than 60 years of age. He was dressed in a full suit of black, with a star on his breast. Mr. Moore acted as interpreter, and the governor readily acceded to my request to be allowed to send a party

---

[16] Letters of Officers of Ships of War, XXV, 407.

into the interior for a few days; a permission which I almost despaired of receiving, for I knew that he had refused a like application some few months before.[17]

Wilkes's movements in the Philippines after he left Manila are described in a letter to the Secretary of the Navy, dated Singapore Roads, February 25, 1842, from which the following extract has been made:

I proceeded to the southern end of Mindoro, and on my arrival despatched the *Flying Fish* to examine Apo Shoal, whilst I began that of the strait of Mindoro. This passage was examined and found to be practicable and safe with ordinary care, and it will be looked upon as somewhat strange that there appears to be more islands undiscovered and unknown hereabouts than in most places, if the charts are to be considered as authority. Those that appear to be known are so entirely faulty in their positions as to make them more dangerous.

Having finished the survey of this entrance to the Sooloo Sea I proceeded along the coast of Panay, having communication with the shore, and making surveys of some of the anchoring grounds; and thence as far south as the island of Mindanao, where I anchored in the port of Caldera, at the entrance of the strait of Basilan. I remained at anchor a day and a half at that place in order to make observations for dip and intensity, and survey the harbor, and then passed over to and through the Sooloo archipelago, and anchored off the town of Soong, in the island of Sooloo, the residence of the Sultan or Rajah. I remained here three days, having friendly intercourse with the Sultan and Datto or Prime Minister, and obtained from him the terms on which he would receive American vessels, in writing, and also a written guarantee to afford all who should have the misfortune to fall into difficulties or be shipwrecked at his islands protection for lives and property.

I then sailed through the group, having fine weather, employed in surveying; passing by the Pangootaran group, and that of Cayagan Sooloo, towards the strait of Balabac, where I anchored under the Mangsee islands on the 8th inst. These two islands were favorably situated for our duties, nearly in the middle of the strait. I immediately despatched the boats on surveying duty, and on the 12th having effected this portion of our duty, I got under way and ran for this port, passing several shoals on my way, and on the 19th anchored in these roads where I found the *Porpoise, Oregon* [purchased to take the place of the *Peacock,* which was lost], and *Flying Fish.*

The result of my examinations in the Sooloo Sea, though not so complete as I could have wished, will be of essential service to its safe navigation and enable vessels to pursue this route, thereby avoiding the dangerous one though the Palawan passage when bound to and from Manila

[17] Wilkes, C., Narrative of the United States Exploring Expedition, V, 293-294.

and China during the contrary monsoon, and passing through the strait of Macassar where they are frequently subjected to great detention on account of the light winds and calms.[18]

The information respecting the Philippines collected by Wilkes is to be found in the published reports of the expedition, comprising twenty-four well-printed, quarto volumes. Of especial interest are three chapters by Wilkes entitled respectively, " Manilla," " Sooloo," and " Hydrography of Manilla and Sooloo Sea "; and a chapter by Dana entitled " Geological Observations on the Philippine and Sooloo Islands." Several charts of the Sulu Sea and adjacent waters were published.

Wilkes's visit to Singapore resulted in the acquisition of much information respecting that port and the environing region. On February 26, 1842, he sailed for the United States by way of the Cape of Good Hope, stopping in the Dutch East Indies long enough to make a few surveys. Until the outbreak of the Civil War, he was engaged at Washington in preparing for publication the extensive scientific data collected by him.

With the advent of steamships in the Far East, the island of Formosa, at that time a dependency of China, lying to the southeast of the mainland, assumed importance to the United States as a possible coaling station and commercial depot. Writing in 1856, Commodore Perry, after referring to its advantages for those purposes, called attention to its strategic position, and pointed out that it commanded, not only the principal commercial ports of China, but also the northeastern entrance to the China seas " precisely as Cuba, in the hands of a powerful maritime nation, might command the American coast south of Cape Florida and the entrance to the Gulf of Mexico." Perry urged the establishing of an American settlement at Kilung, on the north coast. A more extreme recommendation was made about the same time by Dr. Peter Parker, our commissioner to China. He proposed that France should take possession of Korea; Great Britain, of Chusan; and the United States, of Formosa, and hold them as hostages until a satisfactory settlement was obtained of all questions at issue between these countries and China.

In June, 1849, Commodore Geisinger sent the brig, *Dolphin*, Lieutenant W. S. Ogden, to Formosa, to ascertain whether coal abounded there, and if so what were the facilities for procuring it. Ogden visited several ports of the island and established the

[18] Wilkes, Exploring Expedition, II, No. 102.

fact that it contained coal, but he was unable to inspect the mines, as the authorities refused him permission to do so. The samples of coal which he obtained were tested, and they proved to be of excellent quality. The next naval vessel to visit the island was the ship *Plymouth,* Commander John Kelly, which was sent there in December, 1852, to search for some shipwrecked American sailors, but it failed to find any traces of them. In the summer of 1854 the *Macedonian,* and *Relief* of Perry's squadron, under the command of Captain Joel Abbot, stopped at Formosa, on their way from Japan to China, to make enquiries respecting shipwrecked Americans and to examine the fields of coal. No news of the missing sailors was obtained. Several coal mines, however, were explored by Chaplain George Jones, and the harbor of Kilung was surveyed by Lieutenant G. H. Preble.

In 1857 another search was made at Formosa for shipwrecked Americans by Captain J. D. Simms, of the marine corps, under orders from Commodore Armstrong. Simms spent eight months on the island, traveling from place to place, interviewing the authorities, and mingling with the natives. While he obtained but little news respecting his unfortunate countrymen, he gathered considerable information respecting Formosa and its inhabitants. His headquarters were at Ape's Hill, where the American house of Robinet and Company had a commercial establishment. A brief extract from his narrative dated, December 7, 1857, will give one a notion of his experiences:

During my stay at Formosa I made several trips into the country and was always kindly treated. On the 13th of August last, in company with Mr. Markwald, Esq., the agent of Messrs. Robinet and Co., I visited a Chinese town named Pitow, which is seven miles in the interior from Keow. One road took us through a very beautiful country; on all sides were to be seen luxuriant fields of rice and sugar cane; indigo and hemp were also to be seen amongst the numerous productions of the fertile soil. I never tired admiring the beautiful scenery, and regretted exceedingly that I had not artistical skill sufficient to sketch the picturesque landscape that was presented to my view. We traveled in Sedan chairs carried by Chinese coolies, and were nearly three hours in reaching our place of destination. Pitow is a walled town and contains about seven thousand inhabitants. We went all through it and were kindly treated. The people crowded about us and regarded us with a great deal of wonder, but their curiosity never led them to be rude. They are very timid, much more so than any Chinese I have yet met with. After spending a few hours looking about the city, we took up our lodgings at the house of one of the officials who treated us very hospitably and gave us a Chinese dinner.[19]

While the increase of knowledge was a secondary object of Commodore Perry's expedition, it nevertheless collected considerable scientific information. This may be found in large part in the second volume of Perry's narrative. Mr. Bayard Taylor, who accompanied the expedition on its first visit to Japan as master's mate of the *Susquehanna,* contributed a paper entitled " Report of an Exploration of Peel Island." There is also in the volume a paper entitled " Geological Exploration of the Great Lew Chew," written by Chaplain George Jones ; and there are several papers by the surgeons of the expedition treating of such subjects as the medical topography of Japan, the agriculture of China, the fauna and flora of Great Lu-chu Island, and the Chinese method of hatching ducks.

In August, 1852, Congress passed a law providing for the survey and reconnaissance of the western and northern parts of the Pacific Ocean, and in June of the following year an expedition, under the command of Commander Cadwallader Ringgold, set sail from Norfolk for the scene of its labors. In contained five vessels ; the flagship *Vincennes,* Lieutenant Henry Rolando; steamer *John Hancock,* Lieutenant John Rodgers ; brig *Porpoise,* Lieutenant W. B. Davis ; schooner *Fenimore Cooper,* Lieutenant H. K. Stevens ; and storeship *John P. Kennedy,* Lieutenant N. Collins. Ringgold's service as commander of the *Porpoise,* under Wilkes doubtless recommended him as an officer well qualified for the command of an exploring expedition. While he was expected to promote the interests of pure science, his main object was the procuring of hydrographical information for use in the construction of navigational charts for the benefit of American whalemen and merchantmen. He was accompanied by William Stimpson, the chief naturalist of the expedition, and several other scientists.

From the Cape of Good Hope the *Vincennes* and *Porpoise,* under Ringgold, proceeded to Australia and thence to China, making a reconnaissance of sailing routes between those two countries. The rest of the.fleet, under Rodgers, sailed for the Straits of Sunda to make a reconnaissance of the principal thoroughfares in the East Indies. Ringgold arrived at Hong Kong, the appointed rendezvous, in March ; and Rodgers, in May, 1854. Here the fleet was forced to remain several months to

[19] East India Squadron Letters, 1857-1858, 254.

make repairs. While thus occupied, Ringgold received an urgent
request from Commissioner Parker and the American merchants
at Canton for protection, since the Chinese Revolutionists were
threatening the city, and the steamer *Queen,* detailed by Commodore Perry to guard our interests in that quarter was not considered sufficiently strong to cope with the situation. Ringgold
at once responded to the call, and proceeded to Whampoa in the
Vincennes; and a few weeks later when the outlook appeared
more omnious stationed the *John Hancock* and *Fenimore Cooper*
off the foreign factories and landed there one hundred and forty-
five seamen and marines. The depredations of Chinese pirates
also attracted his attention, and he ordered the *Porpoise,* Lieutenant Henry Rolando, to go in pursuit of them. Rolando made
three cruises against the pirates, in one of which he rescued a
large number of starving Chinese, and in another captured, sunk,
or destroyed five war junks.

While directing these operations, Ringgold fell ill with an
intermittent fever, which at times wholly incapacitated him for
duty, causing a derangement of his mind. During his relapses
the command of the fleet devolved upon Lieutenant Rodgers of the
John Hancock, and Lieutenant Taylor of the *Queen.* On July 17
Rodgers, in consultation with Taylor who was then in command,
agreed to furnish Mr. D. N. Spooner, the American vice consul,
an escort to Fatshan, a suburb of Canton—Spooner being anxious
to determine the military situation of the Chinese forces. On the
morning of the following day the gig and launch of the *John
Hancock,* under the command of Rodgers, proceeded on this
errand. Near Fatshan the further progress of the little expedition was arrested by some armed Revolutionists, and the Americans, unwilling to force a passage, began their return to Canton.
At this point an incident occurred which is thus   related by
Rodgers:

> We had pulled a short distance down the stream, when the gig was fired
> upon from shore with a matchlock, and a shot grazed the cheek of Mr.
> Spooner taking off a small portion of skin. The shot was returned from
> both boats and the man who fired from shore was apparently wounded.
> No one else was aimed at, and no other person molested. We quietly re-
> sumed our course down the river and pursued it without hindrance.[20]

[20] Ringgold, C., Report on Movements and Operations of the Surveying
Expedition, U. S. Navy Department Archives, " O," p. 5.

This incident assumed great importance to Ringgold, sick, as he was, both in body and mind, and he administered a severe rebuke to Rodgers and preferred charges against him. He also preferred charges against three or four other officers, and several officers preferred charges against each other. The expedition thus fell into confusion, and when Commodore Perry arrived at Hong Kong late in July he did not hesitate to restore order by the use of rather stringent methods. He convened a board of medical officers to report upon the condition of Ringgold, and in accordance with its somewhat extravagant findings directed that officer to return to the United States. He dismissed Ringgold's charges against his officers, placed Rodgers in command of the expedition, and stopped the execution of Ringgold's plans for extensive alterations of the *Porpoise, John Hancock,* and *Fenimore Cooper,* on the ground that they would be expensive and would delay the expedition. By the time Ringgold reached the United States his health had greatly improved, and he at once made a full report in defense of his conduct and in criticism of Perry. At the outbreak of the Civil War he was placed in command of the *Sabine,* and in 1866 he was promoted to be rear-admiral on the retired list, dying in the following year.

The new commander of the surveying expedition, Lieutenant John Rodgers, came from excellent naval stock, his father, Commodore John Rodgers, having served with distinction in our early wars with France, Tripoli, and Great Britain. By the first of September Lieutenant Rodgers had completely reorganized the expedition and was ready to proceed with the prosecution of its work. He sent the *John Hancock,* Lieutenant H. K. Stevens, and *Fenimore Cooper,* Lieutenant William Gibson, to make a reconnaissance along the Chinese coast and to assist the *Powhatan* in conveying Mr. Robert McLean, our commissioner to China, to Peking; while he himself sailed for the Bonin and Lu-chu Islands and the coast of Japan with the *Vincennes* and *Porpoise,* Lieutenant W. K. Bridge. On September 21 the two last-named vessels parted company in the straits of Formosa, and the *Porpoise* was never heard of afterward, in all probability going down at sea. With the minutiæ of the work of Rodgers's vessels we are not here concerned. Some incidents that happened at Great Lu-chu Island and in Japan, however, are worthy of mention. In July, 1854, the kingdom of Lu-chu entered into a compact with Perry agreeing to furnish American vessels with refreshments and to pilot them into port. When Rodgers arrived at the island four months later the natives refused to abide by the treaty, and not until he had landed a detachment of one hundred men, with a Dahlgren field-piece, and had made a demonstration before the palace at Sheudi, did they comply with the provisions of the treaty. In southwestern Japan, Rodgers several times went ashore to make observations for the purpose of rating his chronometers. He wrote to the Japanese " secretary of state for foreign affairs " explaining the scientific exigency that compelled him to take this liberty. While the natives at times slightly obstructed his movements they gave him on the whole little trouble, and often supplied him with water and provisions.

In the spring of 1855 the expedition began its most important work, a survey of the waters of Japan and the North Pacific Ocean. From Napa the *Fenimore Cooper* sailed up the west coast of Japan; and the *Vincennes* and *John Hancock,* the east coast. Calling at Shimoda, Rodgers found there at the temple of Yokushen ten Americans—five men, three women, and two children—the men having come to Japan with the expectation of earning a livelihood for their families as purveyors for whaling ships. The governor of Shimoda refused them a residence, declaring that the Perry treaty did not grant them this privilege. Interceding in their behalf, Rodgers wrote to the governor that the Japanese government alone could not rightfully interpret the treaty, that both governments should together agree upon a proper interpretation of it, and that in the meantime the Americans ought to be permitted to live in Japan. The governor refused to accept this view of the points at issue, and the little party left Shimoda, going to Hakodate where they met with a similar reception, and where Rodgers made another appeal in their behalf, but without success. They finally returned to San Francisco in " high and just dudgeon."

From Hakodate the *John Hancock* sailed on a survey of the Sea of Okhotsk; and the *Vincennes* and *Fenimore Cooper* proceeded to Petropavlovskii, Kamchatka, and thence the *Vincennes* to Bering Sea and Bering Strait, and the *Fenimore Cooper* to the Aleutian Islands and Sitka, Alaska. In the fall of 1855 all three vessels arrived at San Francisco, and in the spring and summer of the following year Rodgers brought the *Vincennes* to New York, calling at Honolulu and Tahiti. This vessel was literally loaded with scientific information. Naturalist Stimpson, it is said, returned with almost five thousand specimens of animal life hitherto unknown to scientists. In 1857 the office of the United States Surveying Expedition to the North Pacific, with Rodgers as superintendent, was established in Washington to publish the results of the survey, and some valuable navigational charts were issued by it. The Civil War, however, greatly interfered with its work, and a complete publication of the scientific information collected by Ringgold and Rodgers has never been made. The Academy of Natural Sciences and the Smithsonian Institution have issued reports on the Turbellaria and Crustacea and the birds. The invertebrate collections, exclusive of mollusks, was almost entirely destroyed by the Chicago fire in 1871. The birds and mollusks are now in the National Museum at Washington.

In 1849 Secretary of State, J. M. Clayton, instituted a mission to Cochin China, Siam, and certain islands of the East Indies, and entrusted it to Mr. Joseph Balestier, at one time American consul at Singapore. It is recollected that Mr. Edmund Roberts had twice tried and failed to negotiate a treaty with Cochin China, and that in 1833 he had succeeded in making a treaty with Siam. This instrument, however, owing to the enormous tonnage duties laid by the Siamese, had proved to be of little or no advantage to our commerce. The duty of conveying Balestier to the scene of his labors fell to Commodore P. F. Voorhees and his flagship, *Plymouth,* in the early part of the year 1850. The mission to both Cochin China and Siam was barren of results. For his failure at the latter country, Balestier was inclined to blame Voorhees, who, one the ground of the prevalence of cholera ashore, refused to furnish the envoy with an escort. Voorhees was sick at the time and did not enter heartily into the plans of Balestier, for whose worth and character he had but slight respect. From Siam the *Plymouth* proceeded to North and South Natunas, Subi Island, Sarawak, the island of Labuan, and the city of Borneo or Bruni. At the last-named place Balestier negotiated a commercial treaty with the Sultan of Borneo.

In 1856, the flagship *San Jacinto,* wearing the broad pennant of Commodore Armstrong and carrying on board Consul-General Townsend Harris, visited Siam to make another attempt to negotiate a treaty with that country. Harris was cordially supported by Armstrong, who, with a party of officers and a marine guard, accompanied him to Bangkok and appeared with him at the court of Siam.   In no small part as the result of Armstrong's co-operation, the efforts of the envoy were successful, and a new treaty was negotiated.   The duty of carrying the ratified treaty to Siam in the following year fell to the *Portsmouth,* Commander A. H. Foote.   While that vessel lay off the Menam River, she was visited by the " second king " of Siam and a suite of some twenty princes and nobles.   The king said he was the first Siamese ruler to go aboard a foreign ship of war.   He was honored by the firing of a royal salute, the manning of the yards, and the exercising of the crew at general quarters.

Index

EDITED BY ARNOLD S. LOTT
DESIGNED BY HARVEY SATENSTEIN

This book is set in ten-point Linotype Old Style No. 1 with two points of leading by Monotype Composition Company, Inc., Baltimore, Maryland.

Printed offset by Vinmar Lithographing Company of Lutherville-Timonium, Maryland.

Text stock is sixty-pound Warren's No. 66 Antique.

Cloth is AVA 155, Matte, with special PR embossed pattern, manufactured by Arkwright-Interlaken, Inc.

Binding is by L. H. Jenkins of Richmond, Virginia.

DATE DUE

GAYLORD			PRINTED IN U.S A.